WALES:
LAND OF MYSTERY AND MAGIC

By the same author:

Wales Before 1066
Wales Before 1536
Wales After 1536
Country Churchyards in Wales
Radnorshire – A Historical Guide
The Day Before Yesterday
Yesterday in Village Church and Churchyard (Gomer)

Acknowledgements

The following owners of copyright have kindly permitted the use of the under-mentioned items:

National Museum of Wales (on page 30)
Mary and Vernon Edwards, Church Stretton (on page 110)
Mike Rudkin, Michael Bernard Photography, Llantrisant (on page 126)
Wales Tourist Board (on front cover and page 140)

In addition Gwasg Carreg Gwalch have been as usual very generous and most helpful in filling in the gaps.

WALES:

Land of Mystery and Magic

Donald Gregory

ISBN: 0-86381-561-8

Cover photo: Tŷ Hyll

Cover design: Smala, Caernarfon

First published in 1999 by Gwasg Carreg Gwalch,
12 Iard yr Orsaf, Llanrwst, Wales LL26 0EH.
☎ (01492) 642031
Printed and published in Wales.

Dedication

. . . to the descendants of Celts and Saxons, who are still in Wales today, in the hope that they will live in peace with each other, in mutual forbearance.

Contents

Foreword

In writing this, his last book on Wales, the author has had a variety of objectives in mind; to outline what seem to him to be unsolved problems, to expose misapprehensions which have accumulated over the years, to strip off unhelpful layers which have tended sometimes to obscure the truth, to draw attention to matters which appear to him under-appreciated, to spotlight personalities and situations which have excited him, to wallow a little in nostalgia – in short, to enjoy himself and, in so doing, to avail himself of this opportunity to pay tribute to one of the fairest corners of the Principality.

PENRHOS FEILW
Situated south-west of Holyhead is this pair of standing stones, leaning in a field, where their presence has led to many theories, which will remain unsubstantiated until archaeologists dig there.

Chapter 1

Mysteries of the Bronze Age

Despite the triumphant advances made by archaeologists and their interpreters in the twentieth century, advances which have solved most of the prehistoric puzzles uncovered by their previous exertions, there remain a number of mysteries that still await elucidation. Two of these relate to the Bronze Age, the first concerning the intended purpose of those strange patterns carved on stone slabs, known as cup-marks, the other, rather less baffling, has to do with the reason why so many late Bronze Age people saw fit to erect standing stones in very many parts of Wales.

The so-called cup-marks consist of small and uniformly round depressions carved into stone surfaces, which are often accompanied by concentric circles. The fact that there are so many of these marks, both on the mainland of Europe and in the British Isles, makes it the more likely that they played a prominent part in some Bronze Age ritual, though the nature of this ritual is quite unknown.

These cup-marks are to be found either carved on the capstones of neolithic cromlechs or on the outside walls of burial cists or, as occasionally is the case, on separate stones, not obviously used for any other purpose. It is of particular interest that they are often found on neolithic cromlechs, because it provides evidence that early men, whom we tend to think of as pagans, had a well-developed awareness of a need to maintain religious contact with those who had lived before them. Again and again this continuity of religious usage is to be observed in the customs of early people; it must also be borne in mind that the stone cromlechs of neolithic times were well-covered with long barrows, composed of soil and covered with grass, so that for men of the Bronze Age many centuries later to have been able to carve their cup-marks on the upper surfaces of these cromlechs indicates that by that time the cromlechs had lost their coverings of soil.

Of the three chosen sites of cup-marks in Wales, two are to be found on the exposed capstones of neolithic burial places, while the third group had been scratched on a seemingly isolated slab of stone. Not far from the parish church of Clynnog Fawr in the Llŷn Peninsula in Gwynedd is the site of a former long barrow, marked on the O.S. map as BACHWEN, whose Grid Reference is 407498; it can only be approached on foot via a footpath which runs from the churchyard that surrounds this famous old church. There is no finger-post to assist the searcher, perhaps because the cromlech is on private land. An O.S. map is essential. On the top of the capstone at Bachwen the sharp-eyed may be able to count up to about a hundred and ten of these mysterious depressions in the stone.

Our second example is in Dyfed, in a field north of Nevern, near TRELYFFANT; the Grid Reference is 082425. Here there are traces of about twenty-two cup-marks on the exposed capstone. Further east, in Glamorgan, is a stone marked on the O.S. map as MAEN CATWG (G.R. 127974); it lies half a mile north of the Roman fort of GELLIGAER. On this isolated block of stone about fifty cupmarks may be counted. Readers who may want to see more of these marks are particularly recommended to visit Wharfedale in Yorkshire, Northumberland and Kirkcudbrightshire in S.W. Scotland.

The other enigma of the Bronze Age is the reason for erecting standing stones, of which there are still a great many in existence. Some were probably burial markers, others probably indicated suitable routes across country, while others again should perhaps be studied closely in relation to stone circles in their immediate neighbourhood. Nevertheless over many of them a question mark remains. A selection of these standing stones has been made for special mention, chosen specifically for a geographical reason, to enable as many Welsh readers as possible to acquaint themselves with standing stones not too far from where they live.

This tour of standing stones begins in the north-west corner of Anglesey, where three stones to be visited have all been assumed to mark graves. The link between the three is the A5025, which runs from Valley northwards towards Cemaes Bay and Amlwch. About five miles along this road from Valley and half a mile before the village of Llanfaethlu is reached, there is a menhir, a standing stone, close to the road on the right-hand side. It bears the name of the village and its G.R. is 319863. Three miles further along the A5025 turn left at a cross-roads along which in less than half a mile two more stones will be seen, the one to the left of the road, G.R. 333903, the other to the right G.R. 333906; they share the name of PENRYORSEDD.

Two more sites are near at hand, if a short diversion is permissible. One mile S.E. of Holyhead is TŶ MAWR (G.R. 254810) a standing stone about nine feet high, while 1¾ miles S.W. of Holyhead is PENRHOSFEILW (G.R. 227806) where two stones lean in a field about eleven feet apart and about ten feet high.

Back to the mainland and into the Llŷn Peninsula, where there are two more standing stones on our list, both probably marking Bronze Age burials. After passing through Caernarfon keep to the A487 as far as Llanwnda, where the road forks. Take the right fork A499 and stay on it for four and a half miles. Here, left of the road is GLYNLLIFON, G.R. 445541. Take an easterly minor road near this stone which leads to Penygroes. Turn right here on to the A487, where after a further two miles it is necessary to take a minor road to the right, which after half a mile leads to an impressive standing stone, CEFN GRAEANOG, G.R. 455492. As Clynnog Fawr, the St David's of the north is but three and a half miles further on, a further diversion is strongly recommended.

The two stones chosen for a visit to north-east Wales are rather different. First, in the Market Square in RUTHIN on the west side will be found a large, plain boulder around which local folk lore has woven a tale concerning events that were alleged to have taken place in the sixth century. This stone, G.R.

123582 is called MAEN HUAIL. Huail was the brother of the earliest chronicler of Wales, Gildas whose hapless brother, Huail, according to this legend, had the misfortune to quarrel with king Arthur, who is credited with having beheaded him on this stone in Ruthin.

South of Mold on the high ground around Treuddyn there is still evidence of considerable Bronze Age habitation. One particular standing stone is worth a special mention, CARREG Y LLECH, G.R. 249583. For once it can quite certainly be said that it marks a Bronze Age burial site. Further south, a mile or so south-east of Llanrhaeadr-ym-Mochnant on the road towards Llangedwyn will be seen from the road MAES MOCHNANT, G.R. 137248, which almost certainly marks another Bronze Age burial site.

Across country, on the Cambrian Coast south of Harlech is the village of LLANBEDR, in whose ambience there is a pair of standing stones, G.R. 583270 which point the way to the north via a succession of stones, including those at 595305, 599309 and 602313 to MOEL GOEDOG, G.R. 609323. Thus an important prehistoric trading route may be retraced, a route which after Moel Goedog rounded the northern end of the Rhinogs before turning in a south-easterly direction, a stone marking where today the route crosses the A470 from Trawsfynydd to Dolgellau (MAEN LLWYD 707329). The last surviving marker stone on this route south-east of Maen Llwyd is called LLECH IDRIS, G.R. 730310.

Further down the west coast to Machynlleth, the capital of Owain Glyndŵr, who will have seen MAEN LLWYD, G.R. 752008, a tall stone, standing for all to see near his Parliament House in the main street. Of probable Bronze Age origin its purpose cannot now be ascertained. Yet another stone with the same name, G.R. 828005 is to be seen three and a half miles to the east of Machynlleth, a mile south of Darowen.

On a remote windswept patch of hilly moorland, two miles north-west of RHAYADER, in Powys, and a quarter of a mile east of the Old Coach Road, stands a solitary stone, about seven feet high, which experts assign to the late Bronze Age, though why it was erected on this bleak site no-one can now say. Examination of this stone, MAEN SERTH, G.R. 944698 reveals a cross carved on one side, seeming to confirm the local legend that insists that the stone was put up to mark the spot where one, Einion Clud was murdered in the twelfth century. There is however much evidence of Bronze Age occupation in the immediate neighbourhood, an excellent specimen of a Bronze Age axe having been dug up only a kilometre from Maen Serth. The probable explanation is that the cross was added to the Bronze Age stone in the twelfth century.

Further south in Powys, but still in old Radnorshire, is a group of four squat boulders, FOUR STONES, G.R. 245608; they are situated in a field adjoining a country lane, south of the hamlet of Kinnerton and north of Old Radnor. Thought to be glacial erratics, they were brought to this site for an unknown purpose and so mounted that their flat surfaces face the middle. There is a similar group of low stones half a mile to the north. As the neighbourhood is so full of evidence of the former presence of Bronze Age people, it has to be assumed that these groups of stones were their handiwork.

Six miles north of Crickhowell, near the top of the Grwyne Fechain valley will be found yet another stone known as MAEN LLWYD, G.R. 226276. It is best approached – and on foot – from the Grwyne Fawr valley, immediately to the east; keep to this road until Pen y Gader is seen to the west. A path up this mountain leads to this very impressive standing stone, which, it has been assumed, was erected to show a way over the mountains. It is a reasonable surmise that it was set up in the Bronze Age for the purpose suggested. The healthy sceptic however would do well to remember that an educated guess is not always tantamount to a certainty! Back to Crickhowell and on to the A40, where only a mile south-east of the town stands a very tall stone indeed, CWRT Y GOLLEN, G.R. 232168. Though inside the entrance to a military establishment, at thirteen feet it can easily be seen.

MAEN LLIA, G.R. 924191 rears up a few yards from a minor unfenced road that leads up into the hills south of Brecon, between HEOL SENNI and YSTRADFELLTE, its purpose again unclear unless to mark a route. A mile and a half to the south on an even more minor road (gated but quite accessible) is another monolith, MAEN MADOC, G.R. 919158. Standing near the road (itself one time a part of the ancient Sarn Helen) it is ten feet high and has the distinction of bearing an inscription in Latin, commemorating the death in the fifth or sixth century of a Christian Dervacius. Perhaps the best guess is that this was erected by Bronze Age men and used again for a different purpose some fifteen hundred years later.

High up on the moorland east of Fishguard and south of Newport in the Preseli part of Pembrokeshire there are four standing stones of between seven and ten feet in height. Moving from west to east their names and Grid References are: TŶ MEINI, G.R. 995376, THE LADY STONE, G.R. 008387, BEDD MORRIS G.R. 037365 and CARREG HIR, G.R. 064351. About four miles south-west of Fishguard at RHOS Y CLEGRYN, G.R. 913354 is a stone, which stands near neolithic remains in an area much lived in by both neolithic and Bronze Age people. Further south and little more than two miles east north-east of St David's is another such stone, inevitably called MAEN DEWI, G.R. 776275.

Moving eastwards to bring this survey to an end two more stones are listed for visits. First to the Milford Haven area, where a mile to the north-west of St ISHMAEL'S looms up THE LONG STONE. Rightly is it so named; the G.R. is 828076 and the district is MABESGATE, and finally to the coastal district east of Swansea, where not far from Margam, so rich in its past, TYDU, G.R. 802837 is islanded between the M4 and the B4283.

*This is an early engraving, which may well have set the
fashion for subsequent imaginary representations of Druids.*

Chapter 2

The Druids

Much nonsense has been written about the Druids, more perhaps than about any other historical subject; portrayed as men with long, white beards, and enveloped in voluminous white robes they are vaguely associated in the public mind with cromlechs, circles of standing stones and other prehistoric monuments, while the number of geographical locations bearing druidical names is legion. Again in the public mind Druids are especially connected with Stonehenge, where their clones foregather every June to celebrate the summer solstice. Stonehenge, be it remembered, is a neolithic structure, which was erected two thousand years and more before the first Druid set foot on British soil in about 500 B.C.

This widespread ignorance about Druids and Druidism, which has prompted down the years so much romantic speculation, has come about firstly through the Druid insistence on absolute secrecy in the transmission of all information, be it religious, social, legal or political from one generation to the next, and secondly because the entire training of Druid leaders, which took twenty years to complete, was accomplished by word of mouth. Such insistence on oral instruction certainly made secrecy easier to ensure, but at the same time it prevented future generations from finding out much about their religious beliefs, their legal ordinances, their social practices and their system of political administration, though it does appear that they recognised the overall authority of an Archdruid. Of their religious beliefs very little is known for certain, though much has been surmised; their very name has received many and contradictory explanations, the most persuasive of which links the word Druid with the Greek word for an oak-tree, DRUS, persuasive because Druids frequently had their gatherings in groves of oak-trees.

The gap in our knowledge is quite maddening; for instance,

we know that the relatively small number of Druid novitiates spent twenty years at their studies, but we have no idea how these future Celt leaders were selected nor whether some were trained as priests, and others as political advisers etc. Their prestige among their fellow Celts was enormous, their privileges correspondingly impressive, including total exemption from the payment of taxes and the carrying of arms.

These Druids formed the core of Celtic culture at a time when their military leaders, successfully indoctrinated by their Druid masters, were firmly established in western Europe in the five hundred years that preceded the birth of Christ. From the sixth century Celtic outriders first settled in Britain; in the succeeding centuries the Celtic hold on western Europe grew ever stronger until the first century BC, when the armies of Rome, moving north, crossed the Alps and confronted the Celts in Gaul, which was a Celtic stronghold. In a series of well-prepared military campaigns, the armies of Rome gradually gained the upper hand until by the middle of the 1st century BC the writ of Rome ran from the Rhine to the Atlantic Ocean. Celtic resistance in Gaul had been dogged and determined, depending very largely on advice and orders given to them by their Druid masters in far off Anglesey. The Romans soon came to recognise that their Celtic enemies were also receiving help from fellow-Celts, who lived across the channel in southern Britain. With benefit of hindsight, it can be seen to have been inevitable that, when the opportunity allowed, Roman armies would cross the Channel in order to punish the Celts who had gone to the assistance of their fellow Celts in Gaul and at the same time to make a thorough reconnaissance of this northern island, which had not only given succour to Rome's enemies but also provided sanctuary for the all-important priests and thinkers and teachers in Anglesey.

This opportunity presented itself in 55 BC, when Julius Caesar crossed the Channel with a small force of soldiers, which in its brief stay succeeded only in penetrating a few miles inland from Dover, before deciding to go back to Gaul. A year later, a second, larger and better prepared force recrossed to Britain, this time with more ambitious plans, which in the event could not be put into effect as the news of a timely rising in Gaul called for a speedy evacuation.

The Roman invasion proper of Britain had to wait almost a hundred years for it was not until 43 AD that an army of fifty thousand Romans gathered at Boulogne; this was a body of men trained for both the exigencies of war and the quite different tasks of occupation. There was no hurry for the Romans this time; the resistance of the Celts was slowly and patiently broken down, a process that occupied Roman armies for a number of years, though it was only when the Romans approached the mountains of Wales that their real problems became apparent, for it was then that they became fully aware of the fact that Celtic morale would never be undermined until the Druid hold on the Celtic mind had been broken. The further the Roman troops penetrated into Wales, the more they realised that their real enemies were the Druids, who had their headquarters in the oak-groves of Anglesey, from where these mysterious Celtic leaders, who believed in the transmigration of souls and occasionally practised human sacrifice, controlled the minds and the wills of Celtic people. Destroy the Druids, the Roman thinking went, and the Celts could be dealt with piecemeal.

To achieve this aim, a Roman army in 60 AD, under the leadership of Suetonius Paulinus, foregathered on the southern shore of the Menai Straits, their landing craft bobbing about in the water below. The Roman historian, Tacitus, gave a graphic account of the imagined scene, with the Celtic soldiers, whose task it was to defend the unarmed Druids, drawn up in fearsome array on Anglesey's south shore, with the womenfolk of the Druids brandishing torches of fire to intimidate the invaders, who in considerable trepidation eventually made good their landing before pressing on further into Anglesey, where they found the Druid encampment. Here a most barbarous slaughter took place of all the unarmed Druids, an act of insensate cruelty, which was followed by the firing by the Romans of all the sacred oak trees. Too late – for the Druids – the Roman army was recalled from Anglesey to deal with a serious outbreak of Celtic rebellion in eastern Britain, under the inspired leadership of Boudicca, whom we know as Boadicea. The Roman legionaries, after a series of forced marches avenged the rebellion of the Celtic Iceni with terrible severity. Thus peace came to Britain and thus the military power of the Celts was broken, with the utter annihilation of the Druids. Where they make a desert, they call it peace, wrote Tacitus.

Experts differ about the reasons for the Roman hatred of everything to do with the Druids; to some it was the savagery of Druid human sacrifice that most horrified the Romans, whose Senate in 97 BC had promulgated a decree whereby such a barbaric practice was forbidden in every part of the Roman Empire. Other scholars, while admitting Roman hatred of this practice, yet thought a more important cause of Roman opposition was the nationalism implicit in Druid political thinking which was seen to be irreconcilable with Rome's own imperialist ambitions. On balance perhaps the former reasoning seems the more cogent but there may well have been other factors involved in making the Romans root out with such severity the Druid way of doing things. Bards, seers and what seemed to the Romans to be the practice of magic rites had no place in Rome's imperialist planning.

In the Middle Ages all knowledge of the Druids and their beliefs was lost, save perhaps in folk memory, interest in them only returning in the sixteenth century with the quickening of the human spirit which came with the Renaissance, when many scholars had for the first time the chance to become acquainted with classical texts, some of which, like those of Pliny and Tacitus, mentioned the Druids. This awareness of the Druids was probably much greater in France than it was here, but even in Britain by the seventeenth century reference to the Druids became commonplace.

In 1622, for instance, Michael Drayton in his POLYOLBION

discussed Druid bards and their philosophy, while in 1649 the great diarist John Aubrey wrote about Wiltshire, his native county, in the course of which account he described Stonehenge and Avebury, which he said had been built by the Druids. Other scholars in the seventeenth century like Edward Lhuyd, who discussed matters concerning the Druids with Aubrey, were of the opinion that not only Stonehenge but other stone circles were relics of Druid culture, whose priests in Lhuyd's own words were 'our ancient heathen priests'. By the eighteenth century a very great deal of interest had been generated about the Druids, Aubrey and others having fired the imagination of many with the result that gradually the idea gained ground that Ancient Britons and Druids were interchangeable terms and the notion of 'men with white beards and wearing white robes' was accepted.

CAERLEON
Originally known as King Arthur's Round Table,
now known to be the site of the Roman Amphitheatre.

Chapter 3

Arthur and the Arthurian Legend

Only sites in Wales connected with the Devil outnumber those associated with Arthur, who has several burial places and many a stone named after him, along with his spear and his quoits, not to mention the caves in different parts of the country, where he awaits his return to earth, when summoned by Destiny. In addition many a prehistoric cromlech is credited with having been put into position by him. Perhaps pride of place should be accorded to the Victorian diarist, Kilvert, who, after taking a friend to visit Arthur's Stone, a mesolithic site on Dorstone Hill, in Herefordshire, made this comment in his diary on June 26th 1878. ' . . . Opposite the Stone was a rock lying flat in the ground, upon which were imprinted the marks of a man's knees and fingers, . . . believed to have been made by King Arthur, when he heaved the stone up on his back and set it upon the pillars.'

Despite an enormous amount of folklore, which shows little sign of getting any less with the passage of the years, verifiable facts about Arthur are exceedingly hard to come by. It is known that in the first half of the sixth century the Saxon threat to the Celts, which had begun in the previous century when the Anglo-Saxon leaders, Hengist and Horsa, had been invited to come to Britain by the renegade Celt, Vortigern, was held in check for a while by the outstanding leadership of a gifted Celt, thought to have been Arthur. Gildas, whose book was written in the middle of the sixth century, makes no mention of Arthur by name, but virtually admitted his existence when he wrote that he, Gildas, had been born on the very day of the great Celtic victory over the Saxons at Mount Badon in the early years of the sixth century. Nennius, the eighth century learned monk, praised the exploits of this upright Christian leader, who revived Celtic hopes, citing twelve battles which Arthur fought

23

against the Saxons, of which his victory at Mount Badon, was by far the most important. There the historical record ends, there the Arthurian legend begins.

In the twelfth century, just six hundred years after the death of Arthur, there was born in Monmouth one, Geoffrey, thereafter generally referred to as Geoffrey of Monmouth, a town which still regards him as their most illustrious son, despite the rival claims of Henry V, the victor of Agincourt; he received a thoroughly liberal education from his scholarly uncle, the Archdeacon of Llandaf. Thus intellectually equipped, Geoffrey was eager and ambitious to write the history of his fellow Welshmen. His magnum opus, *The History of the Kings of Britain*, was published in 1136, ten years before the birth of another great scholar and churchman, Giraldus Cambrensis. Geoffrey's intention in writing his History was to trace the succession of Celtic rulers from the time of Brutus (having somehow managed to escape from the Siege of Troy), down to the time of his great hero, Arthur in the 6th century.

Readers may well want to know Geoffrey's sources for this book. He was known to be familiar with the chronicles both of Gildas and Nennius, but in writing this book he gave all the credit to another book, written in Welsh, which he said Walter, the Archdeacon of Oxford had given to him, having previously brought it with him from Brittany. All that Geoffrey claimed to have done was to translate this Welsh manuscript into Latin. There are those who believe that such a book never existed and that Geoffrey filled in the gaps of historical knowledge left by previous chroniclers by making full use of his own very vivid imagination, but those however who have studied longest the problem of Geoffrey's sources, content themselves with believing that the problem admits no solution. That he borrowed much and embroidered and embellished more can hardly be gainsaid, nor can it be doubted that the frequent use of his imagination was employed in his attempt to add glory to the name of Welshmen in the twelfth century.

However much critics today may scoff, his book gained an

immediate and immense reputation in the Middle Ages; though it is true that its historical value was challenged by men of the calibre of his contemporary, Giraldus Cambrensis, his stories of Merlin, the man of magic, and of the victorious hero, Arthur, gave the book a seemingly permanent place in European literature. The *History of the Kings of Britain* at once made an impact on those who could read Latin and as before the end of the following century it had also been translated into Welsh, its popularity in Wales grew apace, such was the strength of the Welsh hatred for all things Saxon; for the same reason educated Englishmen, who were probably of Norman stock, likewise rejoiced in the discomfiture of the Saxons, the common enemy of both races.

In the 1130s, when Geoffrey was writing his chronicle, chief interest in Arthur is likely to have been shown by those who lived in the district around Caerleon, the former Roman city near Newport, which, once known as Caerusk, the Camp on the Usk, in Geoffrey's time was called the City of the Legions. Here a grass-covered circular depression in the ground was fondly believed to be the site of King Arthur's Round Table. This legend of the Round Table, which was strengthened by all that Geoffrey wrote, was so universally believed that, even as late as in the second half of the nineteenth century, the Poet Laureate, Tennyson, when planning to write his *Idylls of the King*, went first to Caerleon to see for himself the setting for his mammoth undertaking. Indeed it was only in 1926 that this particular legend evaporated, at least in Caerleon, when Sir Mortimer Wheeler excavated the site and revealed the Roman amphitheatre. See the illustration on page 22. Geoffrey made the narrating of Arthur's career the climax of his chronicle; today's readers, whose certain knowledge of Arthur may be as limited, as is the author's to his achievement as the rousing leader of the Celts in the first half of the sixth century, may well be surprised to read about the truly amazing career of military conquest credited to Arthur by Geoffrey.

Geoffrey described Arthur being crowned King of Britain at

the age of fifteen; he was soon in action thereafter against the Saxons, the Scots and the Picts, whom he defeated near York, before returning to London, where he sought the alliance of the King of Brittany for further military adventures. Together they won several battles against the Saxons, including great victories at Lincoln and Bath. Arthur then marched into Scotland where he crushed the opposition of Scots, Picts and Irish on the Moray Firth and at Loch Lomond. A period of pacification followed in which he appointed rulers to administer the defeated territories; from his headquarters in York he took stock and planned the future. Meanwhile he married Guinevere, who was descended from a noble Roman family; she was, in Geoffrey's words 'the most beautiful woman in the entire island'.

Having pacified Britain Arthur took to the sea and invaded Ireland, where he soon conquered the whole island before sailing on to the Orkneys, which were speedily brought under his control. It was at this time that Arthur consciously planned to make himself master of Europe. First he sailed to Norway, which he overcame, then crossed to Gaul, where he soon laid siege to Paris, which fell to his victorious soldiers. This conquest, however startling, was merely a prelude to other campaigns further south in Aquitaine and in Gascony, as a result of which the whole of Gaul eventually became a province in Arthur's empire. The conquest of Gaul, the chronicler claimed, took nine years. Military success was necessarily followed by careful planning for the political government of the defeated territories. Having pacified Gaul he returned to Britain, intending to hold a great gathering to which all the leaders of the conquered lands should come. 'No prince of any distinction this side of Spain failed to come', there was nothing remarkable in this, for 'Arthur's generosity was known throughout the whole world and this made all men love him'.

These lengthy and quite splendid celebrations, held in Caerleon, were suddenly interrupted by the arrival of a party of twelve men who had come, olive branches in hand, from their government in Rome with a message from their ruler for Arthur, which demanded the immediate appearance in Rome of Arthur himself in order to account for the crimes he had committed against the Roman Republic. The concluding words of this unexpected message were: 'If you fail to arrive, I shall myself do my best to restore to the Roman state all that you have taken from it by your insane behaviour'. The emissaries were listened to in silence and then sent home. Meanwhile preparations were made for the getting together of an immense army with which to counter the threat of Rome. This army, we were told by Geoffrey, numbered one hundred and eighty-three thousand, three hundred men.

The mighty army assembled across the Channel; Arthur first slew a giant on Mont St Michel before marching to Autun, where he won his first battle against the Romans. The Romans then regrouped and received reinforcements, enabling them to offer battle again, this time at Saussy, where Arthur gained a really decisive victory. He then decided to spend the rest of the year in Gaul, intending the following Spring to march on Rome itself. News however then reached Arthur which caused him to change his plans. His nephew, Mordred, whom he had appointed to act as his deputy in Britain in his absence, had, it seemed, turned traitor and usurped Arthur's position. In great haste he returned home and sought out Mordred, whom he several times defeated in skirmishes before fighting a final battle with him in 542 at the river Camblan. Here Mordred was killed and his army dispersed, but Arthur himself was mortally wounded in the fighting and was carried off to the Vale of Avalon – and immortality!

This brief digest of Arthur's career, according to Geoffrey, if treated as a succession of historical events, is really quite astonishing; contemporary writers like William of Newburgh hardly took him seriously. This William, an Augustinian canon, had won a reputation as a wise and impartial historian; he commented thus: 'Geoffrey lied saucily and shamelessly'. Giraldus Cambrensis was likewise discouraging and scathing in his criticism. Nevertheless for many a century the *History of the Kings of Britain* was treated as a reliable and trustworthy history book. Added momentum to this belief in its importance was given toward the end of the fifteenth century when Sir Thomas Malory wrote his *Morte D'Arthur*, which Caxton's new printing press printed in 1485, the very year when the Welsh Henry Tudor made himself King of England. Readers will probably not need to be reminded that the new king's first-born son, born in the following year, was memorably christened Arthur. Malory, who, in addition to being very familiar with Geoffrey's book, had leant heavily on French romantic legends about Arthur, had very great influence on English writers down the centuries, more particularly on Milton, Wordsworth and above all Tennyson.

Geoffrey, as historian, merited the harsh verdict passed on him by the *Encyclopaedia Britannica*, where his book is dismissed as 'one of the most successful works of fiction ever composed'. Geoffrey, however, as the champion of the fables and folklore of his time was the true father of the Arthurian Legend, which did so much to quicken European imaginations in the Middle Ages and indeed in later years too. Of him it has been truly said that 'he had the art of making the improbable seem probable . . . and his ingenious blending of fact and fable made Arthur and Merlin the romantic property of literary Europe'.

ST DOGMAELS
In the parish church at St Dogmaels, a mile south of Cardigan, is an
excellent example of a Romano-British memorial stone, dating from
the sixth century, which commemorates in Latin and in Ogham
Sagranus, the son of Cunolanus.

Chapter 4

Romano – British Memorial Stones

There was certainly a Christian church established in Britain in the later days of the Roman Empire, although in all probability it failed to survive the withdrawal of Roman armies from Britain at the beginning of the 5th century. The resultant return to paganism eventually caused the Pope at the end of the 6th century, that is nearly two hundred years later, to despatch to the shores of Britain his emissary, Augustine, who, landing in Kent in 597, sought to convert the Saxons to Christian ways before moving north to try to repeat his success in Northumbria. All this, of course, is well-known but what is by no means so generally accepted was the success of Christian missionaries from Brittany in restoring Christianity to many parts of Wales, long, long before the official church in Rome took any action.

Earliest and greatest of these Christian missionaries was Illtud, who crossed from Brittany to Glamorgan at the turn of the 5th and 6th centuries and established himself on the Glamorgan coast, where today evidence of the successful mission may be seen at the place named after him, Llanilltud Fawr *(Llantwit Major)*. Happy is the historian who can find convincing factual evidence to back his facts – up and down Wales in the course of the 5th and 6th centuries many Christians at death had their names engraved upon their burial stones. In the 1950s the eminent Welsh scholar, Dr V.E. Nash-Williams performed a herculean task in recording over eighty of these memorial inscriptions. His book, published by the University of Wales Press, *The Early Christian Monuments of Wales* gives full details of design and location of all these inscriptions. They all possess features which help to identify the Christian beliefs of those buried there. Two of these stones bear the Chri-Rho symbol, which combined the first two letters of

Christ in Greek; other Christian proof was believed to be afforded by the presence of various carved crosses and the occasional addition of the words *IN PACE* (In peace), which was sometimes abbreviated to IN PA or even occasionally to PA.

On many of these memorial stones, especially in south-west Wales, in addition to Latin inscriptions will be seen seeming strange groups of incisions in their sides. These groups of notches for a very long time defied explanation but are now known to have represented the letters of a Celtic alphabet which had originated in south-west Ireland where three hundred examples of this Ogham writing have been found. By the middle of the nineteenth century the mystery of the notches had been solved and the meaning of the writings revealed. The fact that there are a number of these Romano-British stones in south Wales that also bear Ogham markings clearly indicates the presence thereabouts of Irish immigrants, but whether these Irish people brought their Christian religion with them from Ireland or were converted in Wales by local missionaries is unknown, though the second explanation seems the more likely one.

It is believed that this form of writing, with no curves or loops, had been specially devised to make it possible for letters to be cut in wood or stone. In Ireland in particular the wood from yew trees was used as a suitable surface for this Ogham way of writing. This alphabet, judging from the surviving examples to be found in Welsh memorial inscriptions, consisted of twenty letters, which were arranged in four sets of five characters, represented by one to five separate notches, either above the line, as in FIGURE 1, below the line, as in FIGURE 2, diagonally above and below the line, as in FIGURE 3, or vertically above and below the line, as in FIGURE 4.

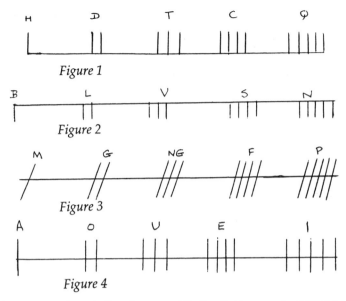

Figure 1

Figure 2

Figure 3

Figure 4

A common inscription began with the Latin words HIC IACIT (rarely the grammatical IACET). This becomes in OGHAM.

Good examples of Ogham may still be seen in Pembrokeshire at BRIDELL, NEVERN and ST DOGMAEL'S, in Cardiganshire at LLANARTH and CILGERRAN, in Carmarthenshire at LLANDAWKE, at EGLWS GWMYN, near Pendine and on CALDEY ISLAND, where there are several, and in Glamorgan at LOUGHOR.

There is also and rather surprisingly at least one Ogham inscription in North Wales. Readers in north-west Wales, who are of an inquisitive disposition, and with time on their hands, may care to search for a memorial stone in a farmyard off the A487, which runs from Porthmadog to Caernarfon. Seven miles north of Porthmadog there is a convenient lay-by on the left hand side of the road; the farm, LLYSTYN GWYN, (GR 482455) is half a mile east of the busy main road up a steep lane. The stone is built into the wall of the farmyard under a lintel of blue stone. The Latin inscription is now almost impossible to make out, though Nash-Williams had been able to give the dead man's name as ICORIX, the son of POTENTINUS. The Ogham notches on the stone are fortunately still quite clear. The visitor is left to wonder how this Irish Christian came to be buried in the far north of Wales and to marvel that his Christian burial in this out-of-the-way place took place well over a hundred years before St Augustine first landed in Kent.

The very best examples of Romano-British memorial stones, both of Latin and Ogham inscriptions, are to be found in museums, where great care and expertise has been taken to preserve them from any further deterioration. Readers are particularly recommended to look at the specimens in the National Museum in Cardiff, and in the museums at Carmarthen and at Brecon. Those however who like to see for themselves the evidence of early Christian burials more or less in situ are now offered a choice of regional locations.

In the eastern part of the Llŷn Peninsula is the large village of Llanaelhaearn, which seems to be crouching for protection under Tre'r Ceiri, the Iron Age 'Town of the Giants', high up above the village, which is about 6 miles north-east of Nefyn. In its church and churchyard are to be found two 6th-7th century Christian burial stones, one, still probably in its original position, is just inside the churchyard gate, on the right-hand side; it informs us laconically that the dead man was called Melitus, while the second stone, now inside the church, where it has been set into the west wall, was dug up in a field near the church. Its Latin inscription indicated that it marked the grave of a man who had belonged to east Yorkshire, which is a long, long way from the Llŷn Peninsula. The attention of those who revel in curiosities is drawn to the words HIC IACET, which provides a rare example of the word IACET being spelt correctly!

Further east again, this time south of Betws-y-coed and on the minor road B4406, off the A5, is Penmachno, a large village, whose parish church provides a safe home for a number of early Christian memorial stones, all of which have been dup up in the neighbourhood. Two of these stones are of special interest, one marking the grave of 'the son of AVITORIUS', adding the information that he died in the year that 'JUSTINUS was consul'. As it is known that Justinus was consul in 540, we know that the inscription dates from the middle of the 6th century. The second stone stands out for another and more remarkable reason: this stone, which tells us that 'Carausius lies here in this heap of stones' has the rare distinction of bearing at its head the CHI-RHO symbol.

Another appealing stone is to be seen at LLANERFYL in Powys, on the Welshpool to Dolgellau road, where it now rests in the parish church. Originally it marked a grave under a huge yew in the churchyard, wherein lay the body of a thirteen-year old Christian girl, RUSTECE, the daughter of PATERNINUS; her Christian beliefs were further attested to by the addition of the words IN PACE. This is a very early inscription, believed to refer to a burial in the late 5th or early 6th century.

Further south in Powys, about five and a half miles west of Brecon, in a hilly area bove the river Usk is *Trallwng* (not to be confused with Welshpool, whose Welsh name is also Trallwng). This Trallwng, a very small place indeed, which lies just north of the A40, on the road to Sennybridge, provides sanctuary in its parish church for a Romano-British stone, inscribed both in Latin and in Ogham. Up to the time of the restoration of the church in 1861 it had acted as a lintel in a window, but thereafter it was attached to the southern wall of the nave, where it commemorates the burial of one CUNOCENNIUS, who is thought to have lived early in the 6th century. The slab has a ringed cross carved on its head, which is believed to have been added in a later century.

Two further visits are recommended in the same locality. First, just south of Sennybridge, lies the ancient Christian settlement of Defynnog, where in former times a Romano-British inscribed stone was secured to the base of the church tower. Today it is to be found in the porch, where it names the dead Christian as RUGNATIO, both in Latin and in Ogham. Its two additional crosses were probably added later. The second goal is a pillar stone, MAEN MADOC, nearly ten feet high, which adorns at a height of nearly fourteen hundred feet above sea level the moorlands, which stretch between Sennybridge and Ystradfellte. This road is a gated section of Sarn Helen, one of the great early roads of Wales. MAEN MADOG (G.R. 919158) marks the burial of DERVACIUS, the son of JUSTUS.

This necessarily selective survey will end with a visit to the south-west, first to LLANDYSUL, where in the historically rich parish church will be found built into the inside wall of the tower a fragment of a Romano-British inscribed stone, engraved thus VELVOR FILIA BROHO; it is all that remains of a burial stone which commemorated Velvoria, daughter of Brohomaglus. Where it originally stood is unclear but at one time, when it was a part of a much bigger stone, it acted as a stile which led into the churchyard, from where it was later taken and placed in the churchyard wall until the early years of the twentieth century when it found a fitting resting place inside the church.

Next to the coast north of Cardigan, in a field, opposite a caravan park still stands an impressive stone, about six feet high (G.R. 289514). It is about half a mile south of Penbryn church. The clear inscription informs us that it marks the grave of CORBALENGUS, who was an Ordovician; this reference to the dead man's ancestry is of particular interest because the Romans had claimed to have wiped out all Ordovicians five hundred years previously!

A mile south of Cardigan in the parish church of St Dogmael's (Llandudoch) is a very splendid burial stone. Between six and seven feet high, it has today a place of honour in the nave, where all may see SAGRANUS, the son of CUNOTAMUS commemorated. In addition to the very clear

Latin inscription, the Ogham carving will be found to be equally outstanding. Though this Sagranus stone may be the magnet to attract visitors to St Dogmael's, it is to be hoped that they will spend more time investigating other matters of historical interest in the neighbourhood.

Lastly, a few miles further south to Nevern, where there is so very much to see. Here however we must concentrate upon early memorial stones of which there are two to be seen. In the churchyard, east of the porch is the VITALIANUS stone, first commented upon in the 17th century by Edward Lhuyd. This 6th century inscription, in both Latin and Ogham, indicates the grave of Vitalianus, while inside the church, embedded in a window cill, is the MAGLOCUNUS stone, again in Latin and Ogham. Nevern, both church and churchyard, has much else to offer to those who love the past and have the imagination to interpret what they see.

Y Faerdref, Deganwy – the seat of Maelgwn Gwynedd's stronghold in the 5th century.

Chapter 5

Bards and Priests

In all simple societies a most important part in helping to bring about social cohesion, so essential to their well-being, was played by the bards, the story-tellers, the men with mellifluous voices and good memories, and healthy imaginations, who entertained their eager audiences with stories on which knowledge of previous times and traditions largely depended. Such well-knit societies tended to prosper and to survive.

Best-known of ancient bards was the Greek Homer, whose Iliad and Odyssey were collections of tales, associated with the siege of Troy and its aftermath. These tales had originally been told by wandering minstrels and were subsequently handed down by word of mouth from one generation to another. It is perhaps salutary to bear in mind that among the various meanings of the Greek word HISTORIA are 'learning by inquiry' and 'the narration of what one has learnt'. History thus came to mean 'the story of Mankind'. A debt is surely owed to these 'oral historians' who handed down in this way the traditions of their times.

And so it was in early days in Wales, after the Roman soldiers left Britain in the early years of the sixth century. These Celts, freed from the centuries-old necessity of looking apprehensively over their shoulders, developed into strong social groups, in which their bards told and re-told, embroidered and sometimes imagined stories out of their receding and ever more shadowy past and in the process strengthened their social traditions.

Of these Celtic rulers who proved themselves capable of taking advantage of the changed circumstances provided by the withdrawal of the Romans from Britain, the most obviously successful seems to have been Cunedda, who is believed to have come down from Strathclyde in south-west Scotland at the beginning of the fifth century and settled with his supporters in Anglesey, establishing his headquarters there at Aberffraw, from which power-base he and his descendants in the following century first crossed over to the mainland of North Wales and later pushed south so successfully that at the beginning of the sixth century Cunedda's great grand-son MAELGWN GWYNEDD ruled an area which extended as far south as Cardigan.

This southern thrust coincided with the arrival from Brittany of Christian missionaries, who settled on the south coast of Glamorgan, where under the inspired leadership of Illtud a monastery was founded at Llanilltud Fawr, a few miles south of modern Cowbridge. This monastery was to provide a steady stream of educated monks, who went forth into Wales preaching the Christian Gospel and where they managed to make converts they set up llanau, where the first Christian groups were formed. This highly successful missionary movement was the abiding achievement of Illtud's monastery at Llanilltud, but it has also to be put on record that in the succeeding years this same seminary achieved as great a reputation for providing scholars as it did for commissioning zealous missionaries.

Foremost among these educated and scholarly monks of the next generation was GILDAS, a Celt who had been born at the beginning of the sixth century, probably in Strathclyde. Later his fame as a scholar caused him to be accorded by his contemporaries the additonal name of Sapiens. Gildas seems to have been in his prime in the 540s, in which decade he wrote (in Latin) an account of wht he termed the fall and conquest of Britain. (De excidio et conquestu Britanniae). Before this bitter polemic against Maelgwn Gwynedd and his bards is considered, the attention of readers must be drawn to this first attack on the newly-emerged post-Roman society, as manifested in Gwynedd. The social cohesion, brought about by strong rule at the top and greatly strengthened by the supporting role of the bards was to be threatened by a new force in society, that generated by the Christian church.

No-one in history has been vilified more than Maelgwn Gwynedd in this account by Gildas but a note of caution needs to be sounded. Gildas' book is the only surviving contemporary record; of the possible achievements of Maelgwn there is no written account, as all we know for certain is Gildas' hatred and disapproval. He chose to ignore any success he may have had as a secular ruler, instead reserving all his invective for the life he led in his court at Aberffraw. Maelgwn's immoral personal life above all brought upon him all Gildas' anger. Occasionally in his verbal attacks he addressed Maelgwn in the first person as here. 'Thou Dragon of the Island, listen a while and hear patiently the following denunciation of thy deeds, wherein I will only touch upon offences, which are spread far and wide in the knowledge of all men'. He continued in the same vein, accusing him of having broken every law of God and man, of having ceased to be a Christian, of having murdered and fornicated, of having behaved so badly that he would have been driven out of any decent society.

There was however an interesting twist to this denunciation in that he also condemned the bards at Maelgwn's court at Aberffraw for praising their master. That Maelgwn had given considerable offence by his personal immorality is fair comment on Gildas' part but his attacks on the bards and their influence is criticism of a very debatable nature, as the task of these bards, along with their essential story-telling, was to help to unify their social group by praising their ruler and recalling the achievements of his forebears. Gildas quite failed to appreciate the role of the bards in Celtic courts and, in addition, even failed to convince his fellow clerics of the justice of his attacks on them. In Gildas' defence however it can be said that in writing his book he had not intended to write a history but rather to wage war on sin in high places. In criticising the bards he was disregarding and minimising their essential role in the development of a secular Celtic society.

41

Gildas, it has to be said, earned his name of Sapiens for his scholarship rather than for success in the mission field; in this sixth century, when he flourished, there were many distinguished, if humble, Christian missionaries who succeeded in establishing their llanau up and down Wales, men of the calibre of Illtud, Cadog, Dyfrig, Teilo, Padarn, Beuno and, of course, St David. None of these devoted men, as far as is known, sought to alienate the bards.

Another cleric now to be considered is Nennius, who lived in the second half of the eighth century and was therefore a contemporary of the Mercian king, Offa, whose dyke was made between 784 and 795. He was a learned monk who comes into the reckoning because he wrote a book (in Latin) in which he traced the course of events in Britain from the time that Julius Caesar landed here until the end of the seventh century. This book, for all its many imperfections, is of value because it was one of the very few books written between the sixth and the twelfth centuries, between Gildas and Geoffrey of Monmouth. He was a Welshman, whose name was latinised into Nennius and he seems to have lived in central Wales, probably near the modern Builth.

There was little originality about his writings, which were closely based, as he freely admitted, on the writings of others. He was a magpie, who pillaged many a nest. Nevertheless he was able to see the significance in Celtic society in the two preceding centuries of the bards, who, he saw, had made themselves a channel through which there passed such entertainment as could be derived from the retelling of tales and the repetition of tribal traditions. In addition matters of everyday importance such as the need to enforce social observances and the issuing of new laws were transmitted from the rulers to the ruled. Nennius not only seems to have been fully aware of the essential part played by the bards but also to have given them his approval, which was tantamount to the blessing of the Church. Unlike Gildas, who was familiar only with social practices in the court of Gwynedd at Aberffraw, Nennius familiarised himself with what went on in a number of courts in Wales, where he watched the way the bards exercised their functions.

He mentioned by name a number of bards, of whom three were outstanding, Talhaearn, Taliesin and Aneirin. Talhaearn flourished in the middle of the sixth century and, as he served at the court of Maelgwn Gwynedd, he is most likely to have been the recipient of some of Gildas' criticism. Taliesin and Aneirin, contemporaries, lived a little later, in the second half of the sixth century; Taliesin probably served the Prince of Powys, whom he seems, according to a surviving manuscript, to have praised somewhat extravagantly. At this time there began to develop an unsuspected and probably unrecognised division of power in Welsh society; for, while Christian missionaries were encouraging the establishment of Christian churches and the spread of education, the secular rulers, the princes, through the medium of their bardic mouthpieces, were maintaining and strengthening their hold on power.

Much criticism has rightly been levelled against Nennius as historian, a frequent complaint being that he undertook a task beyond the compass of his limited powers. To all this and other criticisms made, it may perhaps be added on the credit side that he was successful in throwing some light on the state of Welsh society at a time when the newly-established Christian church was beginning to compete with the secular powers of the various princes.

This chapter opened with the consideration of the part played by bards in early Welsh society, and it seems altogether fitting that it should close with further comment on the same topic. Just as a mother sings to her child and tells simple stories, so the bard, when the world was younger, too sang his songs and told the stories of the past events, with both mother and bard periodically having recourse to the use of rhyme and repetition to round off the telling of a tale. In the developing years of Welsh society right down into the Middle Ages, Welsh

43

bards stressed the relationship of the present to the great events of the past, in particular emphasising the continuity of deeds of valour by their leaders, present as well as past.

Long after the Middle Ages had become merged into more modern times, a process, which in Wales coincided with the accession to the throne of England of the Welshman, Henry VII in 1485, after his victory that year at Bosworth, to be followed just half a century later by the annexation of Wales by England by the Act of Union, the same old stories still lingered in Welsh memories, finding expression in the frequent tellings and re-tellings of myths and folk-lore, hotch-potch though it was of fact and fiction. The surprise perhaps is that all this wealth of cultural experience should have found expression in only one printed collection of Welsh myth and folk-lore, the Mabinogion. This strangely-named collection of stories consists of eleven Welsh tales, derived from myth and folk-lore, history and pseudo-history. It was first translated into English in 1849 by Lady Charlotte Guest, who gave it its name. Readers are advised to read the Penguin edition, first published in the Penguin Classics, in 1977.

GWYTHERIN

The line of four evenly-spaced stones in the churchyard here present visitors with a puzzle. The stones are believed to be of Bronze Age origin, but one of them bears an inscription in Latin, which commemorates a sixth century Christian, called Vinnemaglus, the son of Senamaglus.

Chapter 6

The Siting and Dedication of Churches

The Siting

The earliest and simplest Christian places of worship in Wales came in the wake of successful missionary activity in the fifth and sixth centuries, at a time when Christianity had ebbed away completely from the east of Britain. Devoted Celtic missionaries came by sea, many of them from Brittany, some of whom settled on the coast of south Glamorgan, the best-known early settlement the one made by Illtud who, as befitted one of the founding fathers of the Christian church in Wales, had established not only a missionary base but also a monastic college at Llanilltud Fawr *(Llantwit Major)*. From Llanilltud and from other missionary training centres devoted Christian teachers went forth to spread the word.

In an attempted reconstruction of their activities one may imagine a zealous Celt, having awakened the interest of a few people, who were to form the nucleus of a small connection, took the weighty decision to settle in that place, and proceeded to plant his wooden cross in a suitable plot of land. It is interesting to think about what happened next and to muse upon what considerations were uppermost in the missionary's mind as he looked about him. Security must surely have been of prime importance, protection against man perhaps, protection against wild animals certainly, and equally certainly shelter against the elements. Furthermore he had to find near at hand an adequate supply of water. Thus equipped he will probably have turned next to make himself some sort of wooden hut, before beginning his mission.

Many a missionary in coastal regions of Wales, as he looked around for a suitable place in which to erect his cross on a site, which provided a water-supply and offered rudimentary protection, will have come across a flat area, already well-furnished with his basic needs, where, at first unbeknown to him, other men in times long past had lived their simple lives. These early so-called pagans, who probably belonged to a Bronze Age culture, will have had precisely the same needs as the early Christian missionaries, water and protection. It is hardly surprising therefore that many llannau in early Christian times were established in former Bronze Age sites. Hence it came about that roughly-hewn Christian crosses were sometimes set up in former Bronze Age round barrows. In this way sometimes a start was made at the christianising of pagan Britain.

Gradually men and women will have gathered around the cross, out of curiosity or conviction, and, when a proper connection ensued, a Christian community began to take shape, whose members will often have helped their priest to make a portable altar and also a suitable wooden shelter to protect it from the weather. Occasionally evidence of earlier human occupation will have been obvious in the llannau, and occasionally even today visual evidence still survives of early Bronze Age occupation in a later Christian llan. Three examples will here have to suffice. At MAENTWROG, in the Vale of Ffestiniog near Harlech, there still stands in the churchyard a Bronze Age stone, the Stone of Twrog, which marks a sacred site only a foot from where early Christians chose to build the wall of their church; again, in Powys, south of Rhayader is the village of LLANWRTHWL, whose church walls are but a pace away from another Bronze Age marker stone, while high up on the Denbighshire Moors in Clwyd, at GWYTHERIN, Bronze Age men set up a line of stones, which centuries later Christians incorporated into their churchyard, and for good measure went on to commemorate in the sixth century the death of a Christian by engraving his name on one of the Bronze Age uprights.

All these early Christian enclosures were round in shape, some, of course, having had their shape determined by their Bronze Age predecessors, while others may have consciously imitated them. Let it here be whispered that it is just possible too that some residual magic was thought to linger in a circle! Finally in deciding what the early Christian missionaries might have been looking for in choosing a suitable site, the possibility should be mentioned that they were also looking for a yew tree, whose presence was believed – and with some reason – to indicate the proximity of water.

In *The Holy Wells of Wales* (now happily made available by the University of Wales Press in paper-back) Francis Jones cites over sixty places where there are wells, which were originally near prehistoric stones, some of which were in the fifth and sixth centuries re-occupied by early Christian missionaries. Indeed a well cult has persisted from prehistoric times down almost to the twentieth century. Readers may be interested to know that at one time there were many churches that possessed wells in their churchyards, a very few of which still survive, as at Pilleth and Llanfair Caereinion in Powys, at Cerrig Ceinwen in Anglesey, and at Llangelynnin above the Conwy Valley in Gwynedd.

From the eleventh century pressure of political events in England brought about the beginning of a second important phase of church building in Wales, when the Normans, having routed the Saxon army at Hastings, and captured the throne, soon made clear their intention to extend their area of jurisdiction as far beyond Offa's Dyke as possible. In the centuries that followed the ever-encroaching rulers of England invariably consolidated their areas of conquest by building churches. Hence once again there was a search for suitable sites, but this time with very different priorities. In a district selected for such consolidation the local, and often recently-appointed, lord of the manor, who was either a Norman or at least appointed by Normans, selected a site as near as possible to his manor house. Wherever possible such churches were built north of the settlement they were to serve, allowing the approach from the village to be through the south side of the churchyard.

The churchyards around these new churches were rectangular in shape as were most newly-built churchyards on the European mainland at that time. Norman churches were not normally built in the middle of the churchyard, but nearer to the north wall of the churchyard than to the south, thus allowing as much ground as possible to be consecrated for burial. Indeed in Norman times the only parts consecrated were this south side of the churchyard, the porch and the chancel. The consequence of this arrangement was that Norman financial responsibility was restricted to the upkeep of these three areas, thereby placing a heavy onus on the parish to maintain the nave of the church and the north side of the churchyard, which was to remain throughout the Middle Ages the playground of the parish.

The Dedication

The earliest Christian churches in Wales were naturally connected closely with the devoted missionaries, whose zeal and courage had brought them into being. The fifth and sixth centuries, in which most of these missionary successes were achieved, are often said to have comprised the Age of the Saints. Those readers, who are at all familiar with the dedications of these early churches, may occasionally have been puzzled by the great number of these Celtic saints, more than ninety of whose names survive in dedications of these early churches. The church authorities in Rome, whose power in church matters at this time was supreme, were very remote from far-off Wales and will probably have been quite unaware of the existence of many of these Celtic holy men at work in the Welsh mission field, an ignorance which is reflected in the fact that of all the successful missionaries in Wales only one was officially canonised as a saint in Rome, St David himself; all the rest, whose names nevertheless are always preceded by St, enjoy but honorary status. Their number is legion, but among the best-known were Aelhaearn, Beuno (who taught Aelhaearn), Cadfan, Cadog, Cewydd, Dyfrig, Ffraid, Garmon, Gwrthwl, Illtud, Padarn, Sadwrn and Teilo.

The inevitable changes that accompanied the expansion of Norman authority in Wales are reflected in the way that the Christian church in Wales was reorganised. The Normans, as ardent Christians, were anxious to reorganise the church in Wales in such a way as would commend itself to the church in Canterbury, which now had suzerainty over the latest Norman conquest. Hence those churches in Wales which had hitherto enjoyed their relationship with St David or St Beuno, St Illtud or St Teilo now found themselves under the protection of St Mary, or St John, St Peter or more probably St Michael. A similar pattern developed where with the growth of population following the settlement in Wales of more Normans, the need for a new church arose, when the two saints most favoured for preferment were St Mary and St Michael, hence the proliferation of Llanfairs and Llanfihangels.

A diversion seems here called for to explain the importance attached by very many Christians in the Middle Ages to having churches dedicated to St Michael. In the Book of Revelations it is written that ' . . . there was war in heaven . . . Michael and his angels fought against the dragon . . . and the great dragon was cast out, that old Serpent, called the Devil and Satan, which deceiveth the whole world . . . he was cast out into the earth and his angels were cast out with him'. This 'fallen dragon' most commonly referred to as Lucifer, was not, it seemed, prepared to take No for an answer and has therefore ever since tried to get his own back on St Michael, more especially at the end of every September, when, at Michaelmas, the church remembered the saint. Year after year, it is still believed in some parts of the country, that it is unwise to pick blackberries after the end of September because the Devil in his anger at still being unable to get level with St Michael, wipes his feet on the berries!

Those readers who are interested in church dedications will

have learnt that churches are more likely to be dedicated to St Michael in hilly districts, or if they are actually built on hills, thus, it was fondly hoped, putting the saint in a more favourable position for dealing with Lucifer, the Devil, Satan or the great Dragon. In hilly counties like Shropshire and Northumberland St Michael is the second most popular saint in church dedications, whereas in low-lying Lincolnshire he is only seventh. In England, as a whole, he is the fourth most popular saint, whereas in Wales, hardly surprisingly, in view of its mountainous nature there are three times as many churches dedicated to St Michael as there are in England.

In central Wales in that part of Powys which was formerly known as Radnorshire there was great fear in the Middle Ages because of a ferocious dragon, which was believed to roam around the Radnor Forest. Hence it was that the five churches, built around the base of the Radnor Forest were all dedicated to St Michael in the belief that Christians would thus be better protected from the menace in the hills. The churches concerned are at Cefnllys, Llanfihangel Rhyd Ithon, Cascob, Discoed and Llanfihangel Nant Melan.

In the Norman take-over of much of Wales in the Middle Ages the same renaming process that operated in the rededication of churches will probably have been at work in the naming of wells, but at this distance of time it is difficult and often impossible to distinguish between a one-time prehistoric well that had been sanctified as a Ffynnon Fair in the fifth, sixth or seventh century and a Celtic-named well that the Normans in the Middle Ages rededicated to Mary. Suffice it to say that in Wales from the fifth, sixth and seventh centuries, down to modern times, there have been a great many wells and springs of water which have become very closely associated with local churches, wells that have usually shared the dedication of the churches.

YNYS LLANDDWYN
off the south-western Anglesey coast is the location
of St Dwynwen's well to where pilgrims with problems
in their love lives made their journeys for many centuries.

Chapter 7

Shrines and Pilgrimages

Long before the advent of Christianity a very important part in many early religions was played by pilgrimages, which were made to places, associated in the public mind with the development or popularity of their various religions. There certainly was a strong addiction to pilgrimages among Egyptians, Jews and early Greeks, – and, of course, in very much later times, among Mohammedans, when their founder, Mohammed, who lived in the sixth and seventh centuries A.D., made it an absolute duty for every Mohammedan believer at least once in his lifetime to go on pilgrimage to Mecca.

Many years before this Mohammedin insistence on pilgrimage, however, the idea of making religious journeys of this sort had made a strong appeal to many early Christians, despite the fact that the church authorities imposed no obligation so to do, nor indeed did they associate Christianity with any specified geographical location. Nevertheless many earnest believers, devoted to the memory of Christ's ministry in Palestine, chose, whenever they could, to visit Bethlehem and Jerusalem. In addition, before many years had passed, Rome too became a focal point for pilgrims, with its strong historical connection with the lives and deaths of Peter and Paul. Indeed the pilgrimage to Rome became the pre-eminent pilgrimage in Christendom, once the soldiers of Islam had captured Bethlehem and Jerusalem. (The First Crusade in 1096 was intended to be a pilgrimage to Jerusalem, once the military occupiers had been driven out, a pilgrimage which in the event had to be postponed for many hundreds of years!) Another outstandingly popular venue for Christian pilgrims was Compostella, in northern Spain, where according to tradition James, the son of Zebedee was buried.

In Britain in the Middle Ages the number of would-be

pilgrims grew so fast that, as we read, the highways were thronged with those going on pilgrimage.

Readers may be interested to learn that, whereas dictionaries refer to the origin of the verb TO SAUNTER as obscure, there is a strong tradition that way back in the Middle Ages, when it was exceedingly fashionable to go on pilgrimages, there were many who actually set out but lacked the stamina or the will-power to go very far. Such people were said TO SAUNTER, that is to say, they said that they were going to the Holy Land, but in fact instead of reaching LA SAINTE TERRE they only SAUNTERED! Rome and Compostella will have been beyond the range of most ordinary Christians, but in the course of time the list of suitable places to be visited grew very long indeed, especially as many priests ordered penitent sinners to do penance at certain named sites, where the more gullible among the pilgrims will have had their wants satisfied by less than scrupulous purveyors of pseudo-religious trash. Those interested in the popularity of medieval pilgrimages, are advised to go back to the Prologue to Chaucer's Canterbury Tales, where the pilgrims were bound for Canterbury to visit the spot in the cathedral crypt where the Archbishop, Thomas à Beckett had been murdered in 1170. In the course of the Middle Ages the places most frequently visited by pilgrims in Wales were holy wells, the graves of Christian saints and martyrs and religious shrines which were often to be found in remote places that seem to have made a quite extraordinary appeal to their very suggestible visitors.

Just over two miles south-west of Newborough in the south-west corner of Anglesey lies Llanddwyn Island, a lonely headland which becomes an island twice a day when the tide is full. As recently as fifty years ago this island was indeed remote, the only access being on foot over the sand dunes from Newborough, which today is joined to the coast by a road which leads to a capacious car park opposite Llanddwyn, half a mile away along the sandy shore. Until the fourteenth century the remoteness of Llanddwyn was complete, but in 1303

Edward I, having caused a castle to be built at Beaumaris, and thereafter having discovered to his displeasure that nearby there was a thriving Welsh community at Llanfaes, proceeded to have the entire population of Llanfaes forcibly removed to the western side of the island, where their new home was to become known as Newborough. Two hundred years later, in the sixteenth century, a substantial new stone church was built on Llanddwyn, whose forlorn ruins are still visible today, not far from where the history of the island began a thousand years before.

Sometime in the century that followed the withdrawal of the Romans from Wales, a young Christian woman, Dwynwen sought the security of seemingly inhospitable Llanddwyn and built there a hut and a small Christian house of prayer, necessarily choosing a site near a well. According to tradition St Dwynwen (the honorary title of St was given to all Christian missionaries save for St David, whom Rome officially sanctified) came to the island after an unhappy love affair; in the course of time, from being the victim of a romance that went wrong, she came to be regarded as the patron saint of lovers. After her death, as so often seemed to happen in this twilit Celtic world, the power formerly believed to have resided in the holy man or woman, was transferred to the well. Thereafter for many centuries pilgrims with problems in their love lives made the journey to St Dwynwen's well to gather information about the behaviour of their loved ones. It may however be hard to credit that for many centuries pilgrims with these and other problems thronged to Llanddwyn island where they were required to study the behaviour of an eel (or eels?) in the well. The rather complicated procedure involved sprinkling bread crumbs on the surface of the well before covering them with a cloth. If the ever-watchful eel decided to pull down the cloth along with the bread crumbs, it was interpreted as a sure sign that infidelity had taken place. According to Francis Jones, who is the authority on Welsh folk-lore connected with wells, (See *THE HOLY WELLS OF WALES*) these pilgrims showed their gratitude for favours received by giving generously to Llanddwyn Church, in addition to buying obligatory candles for the subsequent procession to St Dwynwen's shrine, of which today nothing at all remains.

One other description of a Welsh shrine that attracted great numbers of visitors will have to suffice. East of Llyn Tegid and south-west of Corwen in the Dee valley is the village of Llandderfel, in whose church may still be seen evidence of a remarkable celebration in the Middle Ages of the early Christian missionary Derfel, whose name is remembered both in the dedication of the church and in the naming of the village. Who this Derfel really was no-one now seems to know, Celtic imaginations at various times having been fed by stories linking him with knights of Arthur or sometimes even with those who practised black magic. In all probability he had been an early Christian who in the sixth century built himself a simple habitation thereabouts on a site which later became the churchyard for a succession of churches of which the latest is the one built in 1870.

At one time a wooden effigy of Derfel was mounted on the screen itself, which in later days was removed to the church porch, where it sat astride a wooden horse. On the annual celebration of the patronal saint pilgrims from near and far thronged to the church at Llandderfel where it was customary to mount the horse. In 1538 however, two years after Henry VIII dissolved the monasteries, he turned his attention to religious shrines which were to be abolished. Thomas Cromwell, whose task it was to carry out his master's wishes, appointed a commissioner to act on his behalf in Wales. When the official arrived at the church at Llandderfel, accompanied by 8 men and a cart, he was informed that already that day between five and six hundred pilgrims had visited the shrine, but the delegation pleaded in vain with the man from London, even offering him a bribe of £40 if he would leave the effigy where it was. All in vain; the effigy was taken to Smithfield, where it helped to kindle the fire that consumed Friar Forrest, Catherine of Aragon's Confessor, leaving behind in the church porch the wooden horse, where it still remains.

As well as visits to shrines like those at Llanddwyn and Llandderfel and a host of others in various parts of Wales, there were also bigger and better-known pilgrimages to places of special interest to the sick and the curious and the religious. Two of these pilgrimages have been selected for special mention, those to Holywell and Bardsey Island. Holywell *(Treffynnon)*, situated in Clwyd near the Dee estuary, provides the setting for a most bizarre story. According to legend, early in the seventh century, Winifred, a niece of the celebrated Christian missionary, Beuno had the misfortune, in resisting the unwanted advances of a rapist, to be decapitated, but, while springs of water in miraculous fashion sprouted up where her head touched the ground, in equally miraculous fashion Beuno appeared and restored Winifred's head to her shoulders. To satisfy the curiosity of those readers who may not know the legend's sequel, it must be related that Beuno, having rescued his niece, made her the Abbess of a nunnery at Gwytherin, where she was to remain for seventeen years. The parish church in the village of Gwytherin perhaps not surprisingly is dedicated to St Winifred.

St Winifred's well probably attracted visitors long before anything much was written down about its curative properties; the first recorded reference to a pilgrimage was in 1115, since when there has been a continuous succession of pilgrimages, which show little sign of diminishing even at the end of the twentieth century. This well provides probably the best example of a well cult in the British Isles. Certainly in the Middle Ages the long catalogue of recorded cures caused the Church authorities in Rome to take a great interest in Holywell, while its increasing fame can be gauged from the number of visits paid by the Kings of England, from William I to James II. Early in the fifteenth century the Pope empowered the Abbot of Basingwerk, two miles from Holywell, to sell indulgences to pilgrims, while about 1500 Margaret, the mother of Henry VII paid for the erection of an elaborate stone structure over the well.

Interest in the well appears to have been unaffected by the turmoil of the Reformation, as sick Protestants as well as Roman Catholics continued thereafter to take thereafter to take advantage of the health-giving waters. In 1574 a servant, thinking he was unobserved, washed his feet in the well and was paralysed; after this act of desecration he had to be carried twice a day to the well to secure 'the saint's healing forgiveness'.

In the seventeenth century the Privy Council in London, in an attempt to control pilgrimages, ordered its local administrators, the Justices of the Peace of Chester, to close all but two of the very numerous inns in Holywell. Whereupon the Catholic Church bought the two remaining inns and turned them into religious hostels, where Catholic pilgrims stayed and received the mass. Two years later, on St Winifred's Day, November 3, no fewer than fifteen hundred pilgrims made the journey to Holywell.

The reputation of the well went up and down in the seventeenth century; in 1605 Sir Everard Digby, one of the Guy Fawkes' conspirators, accompanied by thirty horsemen, prayed at the shrine, in 1624 an official account noted the large number of pilgrims on St Winifred's Day but in 1630 the Privy Council took a stand and ordered the pilgrimage to stop; this was followed in 1637 by an attempt to disfigure the image of St Winifred. In 1642-3 however the Jesuits replied by starting to build a house for Roman Catholic pilgrims, which they were not allowed to finish. Nevertheless visits to the shrine still went on and in 1683 Mary of Modena, James II's Queen, gave money to the fabric fund and at the same time presented to the officials at Holywell a piece of the dress which Mary, Queen of Scots wore to her execution; three years later Mary returned to Holywell with James II in order to pray for a son. In 1688 James II had to abdicate and his successor, Protestant William III went to Holywell, where he ordered his men to ransack the chapel and to drive out the Roman Catholic priest-in-charge. By the end of the century all the same the pilgrims were back again 'kneeling at the shrine'.

The eighteenth century was marked by general religious indifference but it is interesting to note the comments made by three non-religious visitors to Holywell. In 1722, Daniel Defoe, a staunch Dissident was driven by curiosity to go there but once there, he drew back, preferring to scoff, while fifty years later, Dr Johnson, in the course of his only visit to Wales, descended upon Holywell, where he was disconcerted to see 'a woman bathing, while we all looked', noting in his diary that the baths 'were completely and indecently open'. Pennant, who was there in 1796, was impressed to see so many Protestant pilgrims at the well.

In the middle of the nineteenth century the Pope for nearly forty years made indulgences available to Roman Catholics who made a pilgrimage to Holywell. Early in the twentieth century the flow of water to the well was diverted in part by an industrialist who needed more water to operate his lead mine, but the remaining flow was – and is still – sufficient to attract many pilgrims to St Winifred's well.

Pilgrims to our second site, Bardsey Island *(Ynys Enlli)* may perhaps have first been as much attracted by the island's remoteness as by the sense of security such remoteness imparts in troubled, unsettled times such as those which followed the withdrawal of the strong arm of Rome in the fifth century A.D. As far as is known, the earliest settlement in the island was made by a Celtic monk, St Cadfan, who with his followers established a clas there early in the sixth century, probably in 516 A.D., thus ending a long missionary journey from Brittany via west Wales. Certain it is that there is in Tywyn Ffynnon Gadfan and that two of his followers built the first rudimentary Christian Church in Corwen.

Events on the mainland in the next century greatly helped to swell the numbers of those who sought security in Bardsey; for in 615 after the Battle of Chester in which the invading Saxons from Northumbria destroyed their opponents near Bangor-is-coed, south-east of modern Wrexham, the victorious soldiers proceeded to hack to death no fewer than fourteen hundred unarmed monks, whose crime was to encourage their countrymen by their presence and their prayers. The nine hundred survivors of this, the largest monastery in Wales, with only a bleak future ahead of them in north-eastern Wales, set out on a long trek to the holy island of Bardsey. This wholesale though probably gradual migration westwards of so many displaced monks required much planning, the eventual outcome of which was a well-organised pilgrim route, beginning at Clynnog Fawr, with suitable staging posts thereafter all the way to Aberdaron, the port of departure for Bardsey. Today's visitors will find the most rewarding staging posts those at Clynnog Fawr, Llanaelhaearn, Pistyll and at Llangwnnadl, because in all those places can still be seen vivid reminders of those days.

Clynnog Fawr, G.R. 414409 lies ten miles south-west of Caernarton on the A499. Today's church, probably the finest in north Wales, is dedicated to St Beuno, who had rescued in such spectacular fashion his niece in Holywell; thereafter he had moved westwards and settled at Clynnog, where in the seventh century he built a llan near a well (Ffynnon Beuno) which not only supplied the needs of the llan but also of future generations of pilgrims too. This well at the side of the main road, about two hundred yards west of the church, is surrounded by a wall, six feet high, complete with a seat and steps leading down to the water, which in addition to slaking men's thirsts also acquired a reputation for curing the sick, especially epileptic children. The general practice grew for the sick to bathe in the well in the evening before being carried across to the rush-covered tombstone in St Beuno's chapel, where the subsequent night had to be spent. The popularity of this well-and-tombstone therapy lasted for many a century and it is interesting to note that, when Pennant visited Clynnog towards the end of the eighteenth century he saw on the tombstone 'a feather bed on which a poor paralytic from Merionethshire had spent the whole night'. Beuno's chapel had been destroyed by the Vikings in 978 but was subsequently rebuilt to act as a hospice for pilgrims on their way to Bardsey.

MANORBIER CASTLE
This castle, the birthplace of Giraldus Cambrensis,
happily survives to preside over the peaceful resort of Manorbier.
Of this castle Giraldus had this to say . . . 'Of all the
different parts of Wales Dyfed is the most beautiful . . . and of all
Dyfed the province of Pembroke is the most attractive . . . and in all
Pembroke Manorbier is the most pleasant place of all'. Readers should
go there and form their own opinions.

Chapter 8

Giraldus' Description of Wales

Toward the end of the twelfth century the long-drawn out struggle between the Welsh and the English for domination in Wales had entered a highly important stage, the balance of forces being such that with hindsight those years can be seen to have constituted a temporary period of calm before the storm that was to break over Wales in the following century. Posterity in Wales is indeed fortunate to have had at that time a man of the outstanding calibre of Giraldus Cambrensis to write about the state of the nation.

Giraldus was born in 1146 in the castle of Manorbier, which happily still dominates the Pembrokeshire coastline a few miles west of Tenby. His parents were William de Barri, a Norman noble and Angharad, who was the daughter of another noble, Gerald of Windsor and a famous and beautiful Welsh princess, Nest, the one-time mistress of Henry I of England and the daughter of the great Rhys ap Tewdwr. Giraldus thus was part Norman and part Welsh, and though he came to regard himself as mostly Welsh, his mixed blood did make it possible for him to have a foot in both camps. He once wrote: 'I am related to all the great men of Wales, of either nation.' He was thus able to recognise the strengths and weaknesses of both Normans and Welshmen.

In the Spring of 1188 Henry II ordered the Archbishop of Canterbury to organise a recruitment campaign in Wales to obtain volunteers for the Third Crusade. The Archbishop appointed as his chaplain and virtual deputy his friend Giraldus. This famous journey through Wales in the Spring of 1188, furnished Giraldus with enough material for two books, the second of which, published in 1194, was his *DESCRIPTION OF WALES*, whose purpose was to present to the public a comprehensive picture of what social life was like in Wales for ordinary men and women. Thanks to this excellent book readers today can read a fascinating account of the Welsh way of life eight hundred and more years ago.

Giraldus, it has to be remembered, had been born in Wales, into an aristocratic, wealthy, landowning family; he was three parts Norman and, like many other Normans, he had tended to look down upon and to despise non-Normans, be they Saxon or Welsh. Gradually, however, this racial intolerance, at least as far as the Welsh were concerned, faded away, allowing him sometimes to appear more Welsh than the Welsh.

The first part of his *DESCRIPTION OF WALES*, which is a well-balanced and well-organised book, opened with the repetition of the fanciful fairy tale, linking Welsh origins with the siege of Troy, to which Geoffrey of Monmouth had given expression a few years previously; it goes on to outline the political divisions of the country, to list the genealogies of the Welsh princes, and to describe the main physical features of Wales; in the second part he allowed his Norman blood to do the talking. In it he dealt with what he saw to be the demerits and weaknesses of the Welsh; this remarkable account ended with some advice to the Normans, indicating the ways in which they could most quickly complete the conquest of Wales, followed by suggestions to the Welsh, telling them how best they could cope with increased Norman pressure.

The Welsh, according to Giraldus, were mostly short and dark and very agile; they all, be they male or female, insisted on having their hair cut short, and shaped round their ears and eyes, with their womenfolk covering their heads 'with a flowing white veil, which stuck up in folds, like a crown'. The men favoured moustaches but were otherwise shaven. One and all made do with a minimum of clothing and as a rule ate only one proper meal a day. Giraldus laid particular stress on the attention all Welsh people paid to their teeth, which they were for ever cleaning 'with green hazel-shoots before rubbing them with a woollen cloth until they shone like ivory'.

Begging among the Welsh was apparently unknown.

'Everyone's house is open to all, for to the Welsh generosity and hospitality are the greatest of all virtues'. If a stranger wanted accommodation, he would just walk into a house and hand over whatever weapon he was carrying to the owner, who would give the traveller in return a bowl of water in which he could wash his feet; this was an acknowledged invitation to become a guest. If the stranger refused the water, it indicated that he did not want to stay overnight but rather wanted something to eat.

With such widespread and generous hospitality we rather expect to hear that such Welsh houses must have been spacious; it was not so, as most people lived at the edge of woods or forests in huts which were weather-proof but not much else. Here the harp was played by both sexes and here general singing was usually popular; the seeds of future eisteddfodau were early sown! The singing was not as a rule in unison but rather with a number of parts being taken. In most communities too there was a storyteller, whose tales were told in the intervals between harp solos and communal singing.

Their agriculture was based on growing oats which were planted in April, a month after the ploughing; the harvest tool was the sickle. Their main item of diet was oats, which was eked out with milk, butter and cheese. They did eat meat, however, whenever the chance presented itself. Fishing too was widely practised, often from coracles, which consisted of inter-woven branches of trees, over which animal skins had been stretched.

To complete this seemingly idyllic picture Giraldus added that most Welsh people loved playing with words and greatly enjoyed having an argument; they were, he said, 'quicker-witted and shrewder than any other Western people', but then, in order to achieve some sort of balance Giraldus proceeded to enumerate the faults of the Welsh and to examine weaknesses in their social and political structure. Above all he accused Welshmen (he speaks here as a Norman!) of not keeping their promises and of having fickle minds. 'The only thing they really persist in is in changing their minds'. He then further castigated them for stealing, even from each other, and in so doing 'immediately forget all treaties of peace and ties of friendship'. Politically Giraldus maintained that the Welsh had remained relatively weak because not only were they for ever quarrelling among themselves but they also steadfastly refused to acknowledge one man as their leader. The result of this political weakness was perpetuated by the Celtic law of inheritance, gavelkind, whereby a man at death divided his property equally among all his sons. After this dissection of the Welsh character in the course of which he found so much to commend and so much to criticise, Giraldus loftily adopted an impartial attitude, taking advantage of his own mixed Norman-Welsh blood, grandiloquently to tell all and sundry, be they Norman or Welsh, how best they could compete successfully with others.

First he provided the Normans with a blue-print for completing the subjugation of the Welsh; they were to devote a whole year without interruption to the conquest of Wales, which, he said, could only be achieved 'by patient and unremitting pressure applied over a long period'. Special attention had also to be paid to take full advantage of internal Welsh feuding by stirring up one Welsh prince against another. Castles would have to be built not only at strategic points in the Marches but also deep in enemy country, which would have to be heavily fortified and well-provisioned for long periods. To expedite the success of these policies, it would be necessary for the Normans to stop Welsh merchants from stockpiling from English sources such commodities as cloth, salt and corn. Furthermore to ensure some sort of successful economic blockade, all coasts would have to be patrolled by Norman ships and all ports rendered unusable to the Welsh. Finally towards the end of this year of incessant military pressure, fresh regiments of well-trained infantry would have to be deployed in Wales to harass and destroy. Without the successful application of all these policies 'these belligerent people will never be conquered'. Even so, he warned his readers, the Normans would have to expect very heavy casualties.

This diatribe was followed by another blue-print, this one consisting of ways in which the Normans should govern the Welsh so that they would not want to revolt and, if they did, to make sure that they would never repeat insurrection. Rule with moderation, Giraldus recommended; the ruler must be firm but fair, and must himself obey the law. The Welsh 'respect and revere honest dealing in others, although they lack it themselves'. If treated in a firm but kindly way, the Welsh will want to keep the peace. 'Those who are well-treated and properly recompensed in time of peace will respond more promptly, reliably and faithfully to the call of war'.

The last chapter in the *DESCRIPTION OF WALES* begins with these words. 'I have set out the case for the English (Normans) . . . I myself am descended from both peoples and it seems only fair that I should now put the opposite point of view . . . I propose to give the Welsh some brief, but I hope effective instruction in the art of resistance'. He went on to suggest that the Welsh army would be more successful if they fought in proper ranks and not 'leap around all over the place'. He then put it to the princes that they would be much more likely to hold off the English if they settled their differences with each other and fought as one united army. The Welsh, Giraldus believed, had three advantages; their country was mountainous and therefore fortified by nature, their soldiers required little food and could keep going for long periods, while all Welsh people, be they young or old, were trained in the use of arms. However, while their enemies were merely fighting for conquest, the Welsh were fighting for their very freedom. At this stage Giraldus' faulty knowledge of history betrayed him into saying that the Welsh would be greatly strengthened by the memory of past greatness, repeating the nonsense which had recently been given new life by Geoffrey of Monmouth, that the Welsh were descended from the Trojans.

This homily came to an end with an account of a truly

remarkable conversation that had taken place thirty years before in 1163, between Henry II and an old Welshman at Pencader, which is near Newport, in Gwent, where a battle was about to be fought. The King had asked the old man what he thought the result of the coming battle would be, to which came this reply: 'My Lord King, this nation may now be harassed, weakened, and decimated by your soldiery, as it has so often been by others in former times; but it will never be totally destroyed by the wrath of man, unless at the same time it is punished by the wrath of God. Whatever else may come to pass, I do not think that at the Day of Direst Judgment any race other than the Welsh, or any other language, will give answer to the Supreme Judge of All for this small corner of the earth.'

CASTELL-Y-BERE

Born in one Welsh castle, Llywelyn the Great in 1220 built another, under the south side of Cadair Idris. Castell-y-bere, the Castle of the Spears, must have been a magnificent sight in its prime as even in its decay it commands respect as it reminds those privileged to see it at close quarters of its former greatness.

Chapter 9

Native Castles

The landscape of Wales is pockmarked with well-preserved stone castles, which proudly proclaim their former power and indicate their current value to those who organise tours for holiday-makers from the other side of Offa's Dyke and beyond. Conwy and Beaumaris, Harlech and Caernarfon are certainly impressive and photogenic too – and at the same time anathema to those Welsh people who regard these Edwardian castles as emblems of their forebears' defeat at the hands of invading armies. This chapter however concerns itself not so much with reminders of Welsh humiliation as with the evidence of the Welsh ability to fight back and to delay as long as possible the ultimate triumph of force majeure.

The Welsh also learned how to build in stone, their first such castle probably being the one at Dolwyddelan (G.R. 722524) where its ruined tower still continues to dominate the gaunt landscape as the A470 climbs up a mile beyond the village of the same name of its way to Blaenau Ffestiniog. Here in 1170 or thereabouts this first Welsh stone castle of any note was built, the credit for the achievement going to Iorwerth Drwyndwn, *Iorwerth of the Broken Nose;* three years later this son, Llywelyn ap Iorwerth was born, and here in this lonely stronghold in the hills Wales' great hope for the future spent much of his boyhood. In 1194 he became Prince of Gwynedd; before he died in 1240 he had richly deserved the title given him by his appreciative fellow-countrymen of Llywelyn Fawr, *Llywelyn the Great.* At the time of his death it was fondly believed that those who succeeded him would be able to achieve the full independence of Wales, for which Llywelyn Fawr had laid apparently firm foundations.

Half a mile south-east of Llanberis on the western side of Llyn Peris stands the stone tower of Dolbadarn Castle

(G.R. 585595) some forty feet high, where in the last years of the twelfth or the early years of the thirteenth century Llywelyn ap Iorwerth, son of the builder of Dolwyddelan castle, emulated his father's achievement by erecting a stout fortress as protection against all his enemies. In the event it seems to have been more useful as a prison for those who fell foul of the castle's owners. Here, according to the sixteenth century antiquary, John Leland, Llywelyn ap Gruffudd, the grandson of Llywelyn ap Iorwerth, saw fit to imprison for twenty years his elder brother Owain Goch. Later a younger brother Dafydd lived in the castle for a while until driven out by the Earl of Pembroke, who then handed over the castle to Edward I. In the following century its ownership must have reverted to the Welsh because in 1401 Owain Glyndŵr, in the course of his meteoric rise to power, held in the castle at Dolbadarn his archenemy, Lord Gray of Ruthin until such time as a substantial ransom was paid. In its prime the castle had, in addition to the tower that still survives, two other equally imposing towers, all linked together with a curtain wall four feet thick. The Welsh by this time had clearly learnt too how to build strong points.

Having described two Welsh success stories in the art of building castles in stone, it seems only fair to make mention of another castle, which enjoyed only a short and chequered history. A thousand feet above sea level and three-quarters of a mile north-east of Llangollen stands a hill with a conical summit, which is often a welcome sign to visitors by road that they are getting near Llangollen. On the top of this isolated hill in Iron Age times was sited a hill fort, whose earthen ramparts and ditches may still be traced by those who stand on the summit, from which vantage point there is also a splendid view of the whole Vale of Llangollen. Some time in the second half of the thirteenth century, probably in 1270, a stone castle was built on this summit around which in former centuries Iron Age people had built their settlement. Dinas Brân was probably built by Gruffudd ap Madog, whose father was responsible for the building of the Cistercian Abbey of Valle Crucis down below in a meadow beside the river Dee. The life of this castle lasted but seven years and is unchronicled save for the sad fact that it was destroyed by fire in 1277. It appears that thereafter no attempt was made to rebuild Dinas Brân.

Of Ewloe castle Jan Morris wrote: 'It is the most secretive of castles, hidden away in its dell like a robbers' hideaway.' Its Grid Reference is 292674 and it is to be found north of Ewloe on high wooded land which the Welsh chose as a suitable location for dealing with any attack on N.E. Wales which English invaders might mount. From today's assortment of ruins among the trees and undergrowth a picture emerges of a one-time strong defensive position, which was originally believed to have been constructed by Llywelyn ap Gruffudd (the Last) in or shortly after 1257; this view has since been corrected by the realisation that the so-called Welsh Tower, which stands in the very middle of the ruins was in fact of earlier construction, probably the handiwork of none other than Llywelyn ap Iorwerth himself. Apparently a surprise attack by English forces succeeded in capturing the Welsh Tower, which was recaptured in 1257 by the Welsh, under the leadership of Llywelyn ap Gruffudd, who immediately set about rebuilding and strengthening the fortification by adding other towers and securing them all with curtain walls. In this quiet woodland setting it is interesting today to remember that the two greatest Welsh leaders of the twelfth and thirteenth centuries made their complementary contributions to the building of Ewloe castle.

Castell y Bere, *the Castle of the Spears,* enjoys a dramatic and spectacular location under the formidable south side of Cadair Idris, about seven miles north-east of Tywyn and twelve miles south of Dolgellau. One of the largest and most important of native Welsh castles, it was begun in about 1220 by none other than the great Llywelyn ap Iorwerth, its function to protect Gwynedd from all comers and especially from the English. For a long time it served its purpose but everything was to change when Llywelyn's grandson, Llywelyn ap Gruffudd was killed in 1282; his brother Dafydd withdrew to Castell y Bere, from which he had to flee in the following year, when an English army marched up the Dysynni valley and took the castle by storm. Thereafter the new occupant Edward I strengthened the castle, having another tower built at the southern end and joining it to the earlier north tower by a substantial curtain wall. However, events elsewhere determined that its active life was over as the English contingent had to evacuate the castle but before so doing inflicted such severe damage to it that the Welsh would never be able to rebuild it. Few castles today do more to reward the imaginative student more generously than does Castell y Bere, where the past still comes most vividly alive.

Further north, on the coast, west of Porthmadog, and overlooking Tremadog Bay, Cricieth preens itself, the focus of attention today for those whose enthusiasm for everything to do with David Lloyd George takes them to the nearby village of Llanystumdwy whereas to those whose interest in the struggle of Welshmen in the Middle Ages to make themselves independent of government by London the very centre of Cricieth is the focus of attention; for there, on the most seaward of the two rounded little hills in about 1230 the Welsh built a sturdy stone castle, at a time when the Welsh star was in the ascendant with Llywelyn Fawr in his prime. The builders had carefully selected a site so close to the sea that in an emergency the Welsh garrison could be provisioned by water. Half a century later, in 1282, the dreadful year when the Welsh dream of independence suddenly evaporated, Llywelyn ap Gruffudd, grandson of Llywelyn Fawr, was murdered; whereupon the English king, Edward I, in carrying out his plan for securing north Wales for the English crown by building stout castles, such as those that emerged at Conwy, Beaumaris, Caernarfon and Harlech, also proceeded to Cricieth, where he took over the castle which he then greatly strengthened. Thereafter the story of the Welsh struggle to gain their independence was a sorry one save for a brief intermission of hope in 1404 when the meteoric Owain Glyndŵr captured Cricieth castle and for a short while held it against all comers.

Dolforwyn, the last to be built of the native Welsh castles, was the brain-child of Llywelyn ap Gruffudd; built in 1273, it was set on a ridge four hundred feet above the Severn, four miles north-east of Newtown, in Powys, and close to today's village of Abermule. Edward I had succeeded to the throne of England in 1272 and it was Llywelyn's intention to show the King that the Prince of Gwynedd was not a man to be trifled with. Hence the choice of a site for a castle close to the English headquarters in Montgomery castle, only five miles to the east of Dolforwyn. In its very short life of four years (Edward I destroyed Dolforwyn in 1277), a small town had begun to crystallise under the walls of the castle. Today's visitors, while admiring the strategic situation of the castle, will find little evidence of its former existence, save for a walled enclosure, which covers an area of about two hundred and forty feet by ninety feet, below which may be spotted in the grass a platform and a number of well-grassed humps, which probably cover a few buildings in the small town under the walls.

The story of native Welsh castle-building, especially in south Wales, developed against the background of the long and bitter struggle of Welsh princes against each other for supremacy. Had they been able to settle their differences, the task of attempting to unify Wales would have been incomparably less difficult, as it would have been impossible for their would-be English conquerors to play off one Welsh faction against another.

Of early Welsh-built castles in south Wales pride of place must go to Dinefwr, which the English call *Dynevor* (G.R. 611218). There, in the ninth century ruled Rhodri, rightly called the Great, a contemporary of Alfred the Great. At Dinefwr Rhodri successfully laid the foundations for a union of the disparate princedoms of Wales. His seat of power was on a hill, one mile west of Llandeilo, where, along with another early castle, that at Dryslwyn, a few miles further west, the effective control over the Tywi valley was maintained. Again, in the eleventh century, Dinefwr was important, when the ruler was Rhys ap Tewdwr, reaching its peak of achievement in the early years of the twelfth century under Rhys ap Gruffudd, the future Lord Rhys. In the next century Henry III lost an army of three thousand Englishmen, who were all killed in an abortive attempt to capture the castle, though later in the century, in 1276, Dinefwr did pass for a few years into English hands. Amid all the splendours of the park at Dinefwr today discerning visitors would do well to spare a glance for a ruined stone keep of the earlier castle, where the Lord Rhys once held sway.

THE YEW AT ST DOGMAELS

*St Dogmaels has already been mentioned in connection with the
Romano-British memorial stone preserved in the church but it has in
addition other claims to fame, which include the now-ruined
St Mary's Abbey, which was built in the churchyard of the parish
church. In the small space between the south door of the parish church
and the north entrance to the abbey ruins stands this yew tree. Note
that it needs a brick wall three feet high to contain it.*

Chapter 10

Yew Trees

The immense significance of yew trees in the story of Wales is clearly indicated by the realisation that of the seventy churchyards there that possess yew trees that are more than a thousand years old, more than thirty of them have trees which were growing in their present positions before Christian churchyards were consecrated around them. The yew tree, one of the relatively few native trees in Britain, was sacred to the Celts, who first arrived in Wales in about 500 B.C.; its great age has, according to experts in this field, come about as the result of its truly remarkable ability to regenerate itself, its branches, when left alone for a long time, bend down and bury themselves in the ground, where they take root and in the fullness of time circles of new trees are formed. Early prehistoric people could well have built their sacred places in conscious imitation of the natural circular groves of yew trees, which they saw all around them. It seems highly probable that the magic properties that were associated with the yew arose from its astonishing ability to regenerate itself. There are many areas of Wales where ancient yew trees are certainly older than the churchyards they now adorn; two such areas have been selected for special mention in each of which a short excursion will reveal two excellent examples, one such site being in Powys, the other in Clwyd.

The Powys excursion involves a visit to Llanfihangel Nant Melan and Discoed, whose churches, originally dedicated to early Celtic Christian missionaries, were rededicated by the Normans who put them under the protection of St Michael, whose influence was hoped to be helpful in dealing with a fierce dragon which was believed to roam on the Radnor Forest, that looms above both settlements. Llanfihangel Nant Melan (G.R. 180582) is situated on the A44, about two and a half miles west of New Radnor. Today's church, virtually rebuilt in 1846,

81

occupies the same site as the original building inside a circle of yew trees, of which eight have survived; at the foot of one of these is to be found a large stone, four feet high and two feet wide. This has been classified as a Bronze Age burial site, one of many to be found in that part of the former Radnorshire.

Discoed (G.R. 277647) lies about ten miles to the north-east, on a minor road. Here, in today's round churchyard, was another prehistoric settlement, of which the evidence is of a large mound near the church and two huge old yews, their great age attested to by their girth of thirty-seven feet. These same trees will have witnessed many centuries later the building of a Christian church, whose builder, a Celtic Christian missionary, chose to use for Christian worship a burial place, previously sanctified by prehistoric men and women. Discoed's surviving yews still bear witness to the continuity of religious association thereabouts.

The first churchyard to be visited on the second excursion – to Clwyd – is at Llangernyw, (G.R. 876674) which is situated on the A548 between Llanfair Talhaearn and Llanrwst. Here once again there is a circle of yew trees in a round churchyard, whose church stands on a former Bronze Age site, which is presided over by a great yew, just north of the church, its massive circumference being more than thirty-four feet.

Five miles south of Llangernyw, on a minor road, B5384, is the ancient settlement of Gwytherin, (G.R. 877614) in whose round churchyard are several very large yews, two of which are about twenty-six feet in girth. On the north side of the churchyard is a real surprise, an alignment of Bronze Age standing stones, near the yews. On the most westerly of the prehistoric stones a Latin inscription commemorates the death of an early Celtic Christian, Vinnemaglus, the son of Senemaglus. This is another excellent example of the continuity of religious usage, the unifying genius of both the pre-Christian and the Christian settlement being the old yew trees.

The first Welsh Christians, who had been converted by missionaries, mainly from Brittany in the 5th century, already held yew trees in high regard. Their acceptance of the magic powers associated with these trees probably preceded their acceptance of Christian principles. This respect for the yew lay deeply embedded in their Welsh consciousness, so that when Christian missionaries built their first simple religious buildings, as they often did on sites, already occupied by yew trees, their converts found their veneration for the trees greatly strengthened.

Years later, after St Augustine had succeeded in making Christian Anglo-Saxon England, the newly-converted Saxons, though not necessarily accepting the Celtic attitude to the magic of the yew, yet developed the habit of planting a yew at the entrance to the churchyard, which was generally on the south side of the church. Later still, after the Norman conquest, as the new masters gained the upper hand in parts of what is now known as Gwent and Glamorgan, the Saxon habit of planting a yew at the entrance to the churchyard, spread westwards. In the Book of Llandaf, a 12th century inventory of land, reference is made to the right of sanctuary in Wales extending from 'the yew tree by the gate to the church door'. In addition the right to store household goods temporarily under churchyard yews was granted to those who sought sanctuary in the churchyard.

Tales of the magic exercised by the yew have accumulated down the years in Wales and readers may be amused to know of one such tale that circulated in the northern part of Radnorshire little more than two hundred years ago. In those happy pre-television days ordinary folk tended to make their own amusement, in the pursuit of which they developed strong local partisanship, as in the case now to be reported. There was at that time a doughty exponent of the art of fisticuffs who lived in Newtown; he was up to that time unbeaten and generally regarded as unbeatable. The time came however when a daring upstart from the little village of Llanbadarn Fynydd, south of Newtown, mounted a challenge which the champion readily accepted. The coming contest aroused great interest in the valleys and it was decided that such a popular fight had to be fought on neutral ground, which was provided by another village to the east of Llanbadarn, namely Beguildy, in the upper Teme valley. An excited gathering in the local churchyard witnessed a fierce fight develop, which, to the astonishment of the bystanders began to go the way of the Llanbadarn man. In the end the Newtown champion did indeed bite the dust. The reason for this quite unexpected outcome was forthcoming only when one of the spectators, who was more observant than the rest, had noticed that in the yew tree not far from the fight the local vicar of Beguildy was crouching in the branches 'with a huge book opened in front of him, directing the evil spirits to assist the man from Llanbadarn'. Truly it is not the truth that matters but what you believe to be true!

Whatever the origin of the yew in the churchyard, it played a prominent part in the life of the parish in the Middle Ages and in some places like Beguildy later on too! Mention has already been made of its role in providing sanctuary and much has been written about its value in providing the parish with a supply of bows in an emergency, although it seems unlikely that in Wales as much use was made of this opportunity as in some other parts. It has too to be said that those who had the reputation of being the best bowmen of Wales, the men of Gwent, preferred to make their weapons of elm rather than of yew. All the same of the general usefulness of the yew in making possible the manufacturing of bows there can be little doubt. It is interesting to note that, when in 1991 a Neolithic corpse was discovered high up in the Dolomites near the border between Italy and Austria, it was found to have been almost miraculously preserved, thanks to the permafrost. This Iceman, as the papers called him, this 5000 year-old survivor of the New Stone Age had at his side a bow, six feet long; it was made of yew.

Back to the Middle Ages, when in 1307 Edward 1st, in an act of parliament, ordained that churchwardens of parish churches should see to it that groups of yew trees should be planted in front of church porches, in order to protect the fabric from high winds and storms. In the run up to Easter the yew again had a part to play; for, on Ash Wednesday the faithful, in an act of contrition, smeared their foreheads with the ash of charred yew twigs, and, again in Lent, on Palm Sunday, when Christians commemorated Christ's triumphant ride into Jerusalem, parishioners in procession normally carried branches of hazel catkins in imitation of the unobtainable palms, but in the years, in which Easter was so late that catkins were unavailable, the yew once again was on hand to be of service to the parish.

Readers who are familiar with the village of Aberedw, south of Builth, in Radnorshire will remember the two very large yew trees that stand quite close to the north door of the church. Here, as recently as in Victorian times, according to the local record, on the occasion of the annual patronal festival no fewer than sixty couples managed to dance between the watchful yews, to the accompaniment of music, provided by parishioners who fiddled away in the nearby and very capacious church porch.

It is invidious to particularise but some selection has been inevitable; it has however to be stressed that no students of Welsh yews can feel that they have done justice to their subject until they have seen most of the following sites of yews, none of which however have managed to find their way into this text: – Betws-y-coed (old church), Caerhun, Capel-y-ffin, Cascob, Cefnllys, Defynnog, Gresford, Llanarth, Llanbadarn Fawr (Dyfed), Llanddeiniolen, Llanfair Discoed, Llanfaredd, Llangadwaladr, Llangollen, Llanrhidian, Llansilin, Maentwrog, Overton, Pennant Melangell and Rhulen.

LLANDDEWI CHURCH, GOWER

*Above the porch on Llanddewi church, which is to be found on a
minor road between Rhosili and Llangennith, will be seen – with some
difficulty – a rare medieval sun-dial; – with difficulty because the dial
is partly obscured by the lamp beneath it.*

Chapter 11

Medieval Sun Dials

Today our lives are controlled and dominated by the time, an alarm, be it mechanical or electric, from clock or telephone, from radio or television, for many of us starting our day, whose every activity thereafter will be determined by the time, which is anxiously and continually scrutinised throughout the day by consulting watch or clock, radio or television. So much for the much-vaunted freedom of our civilized life.

Time was however, and not so many centuries ago when the lives of those who lived before us depended solely on the rising and the setting of the sun; most people arose with the sun and went to bed when the sun set or soon after. In these islands the need to know the time and therefore the impetus to find means of determining it was greatly increased by the establishment of the Christian church, whose success at the local level would never have been obtained if people had not known at what time the services were held. Hence the need arose for the church authorities to provide some simple means for Christians to know the time to enable them to attend mass; the first attempts in our early British societies, be they Celtic or Saxon to inform the people of the time was made by priests so that the time when masses were said were generally known in the locality. However very few pre-Norman sun-dials have survived and those few date only from the century immediately preceding the Norman invasion. Indeed only ten such dials have survived in eastern Britain, while only one has been found in Wales.

Surmise about the reason for this dearth takes the place of certainty; what however is true is that most pre-Norman churches were of a very flimsy construction and had therefore in the course of time either to be strengthened or abandoned and a new church built in its place. This fact, however true, offers no proof that many dials existed on the original churches.

These first sun-dials on pre-Norman churches consisted of a long horizontal line scratched on the stone, the beginning of which represented dawn and the end sunset. Half way along this scratched line a hole in the stone was made, from which another scratched line was carved at right-angles to the horizontal one. Either side of this line, which marked midday, other lines were scratched, marking 9 a.m. and 3 p.m. In the centrally-placed hole an iron marker, known as a gnomon, was inserted whose shadow at midday marked noon. See the diagram.

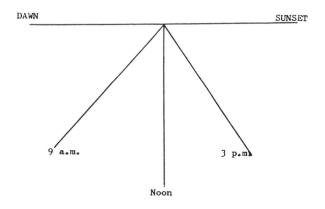

Pre-Norman Sun-Dial

The sole surviving known specimen in Wales of a Celtic pre-Norman dial can still be seen in the churchyard of Clynnog Fawr in the Llŷn peninsula, known to many as the St David's of North Wales. Those familiar with the splendours of Clynnog Fawr may be forgiven if the sight of this sun-dial has escaped them, as there is so much else to be seen there and thereabouts to capture the attention of archaeologists, historians and indeed of all who are imaginatively involved in the study of the past. About six feet south-west of St Beuno's chapel is a free-standing pillar stone on which has been carved a simple sun-dial, marking the main times of mass; it is hard to date accurately but is thought to be the second oldest churchyard dial in these islands.

The need for more local sun-dials grew after the Norman Conquest as the population increased; hence it was that between the 12th and the end of the 15th centuries a great many sun-dials were scratched on church walls, especially in those many areas where no clocks had yet made their appearance. The earliest cathedral clock, that at Canterbury did not appear until the 13th century. This second type of sun-dial, usually referred to as a scratch dial, generally consisted of a full circle with a hole in the centre for a gnomon. Nowhere was the expansion in the number of such dials as remarkable as in the southern parts of the Cotswolds, where in south Gloucestershire around Cirencester a remarkable number of scratch dials may still be seen, many churches actually having two, three or even more specimens. The impression, however erroneous, is given of succeeding generations of villagers thinking to improve upon the dials scratched by their grandparents! Yet, despite the universal need to know the time, there are parts of the country where no examples have survived, the explanation probably being the widespread incidence of erosion in some districts, and in others lack of building skills may have made rebuilding essential. In some districts a careful search of external walls today will sometimes reveal blocks of stone, which had formerly carried the tell-tale scratches, having since been re-used purely as building bricks, with parts of the scratched dial still visible, often in an upside-down position!

During these later medieval years scratch dials will have appeared on many Welsh churches too but in many years of searching by the author on all southern walls no more than three of these dials have ever been found. It is quite possible that more have escaped the ravages of time, but natural erosion, combined with poor building techniques, will probably have accounted for the obliteration of many examples. First of the three Welsh survivors is at Ewenny in Glamorgan, about a mile and a half south of Bridgend; this former Benedictine Abbey is the best example of an early Norman church in the whole of Wales. On the south outside wall of the south transept is a good example of a scratch dial, which marked the times of the four principal services.

For a sight of the two other medieval scratch dials a visit to the Gower peninsula is called for; where the road to Worms Head ends, stands the village of Rhosili. This is the second village of that name in the peninsula, as the earlier one disappeared into the sand dunes in the early years of the fourteenth century. After this disaster the new Rhosili church was built later in the same century, in the porch of which may be seen a scratch dial, whose presence there is more decorative than useful. This perhaps surprising situation arose when the builders of the new church managed to rescue from the dunes the scratch dial from the earlier church and found a home for it in the new building. Retracing our steps about four miles inland, from Rhosili, the village of Llanddewi will be found on a minor road; its parish church bears a medieval scratch dial on the porch, where today it is partly obscured by a lamp (see the illustration).

After the Reformation church walls were not usually used for sun-dials; from then until the nineteenth century, when the practice of placing sun-dials in churchyards generally ceased, horizontal metal dials were set on top of former churchyard crosses, which Protestant zealots in the early years of the Reformation caused to be stumped. Many examples of this third type of sun-dial are still to be found in Welsh churchyards.

CONWY CASTLE
Pennant in describing John Williams' boyhood in Conwy, wrote this.
' . . . in his childish years with other playmates he was diverting
himself with leaping from parts of the wall of Conwy down to the
shore. The fall was on so critical a part as ever to secure him from all
reproaches of unchastity.'

Chapter 12

A Welsh Family in 17th Century London

It has ever been a human characteristic, when times have been hard, to pack up and leave the countryside and make for the big town, London in particular being the goal for many such, who perhaps sought security in numbers or who at least believed that the capital had more jobs to offer. And so it was with a young Welshman, John ap Henry, who had been born in 1590, in the reign of the first Elizabeth; his home town in south Glamorgan was Briton Ferry, where the first settlement had been made in the twelfth century by the Normans, who organised a ferry there across the river Neath. John ap Henry (his father called himself Henry Williams), in early adulthood finding little prospect of making a living locally did what so many of his fellow countrymen have always done and migrated to London, hoping thereby to improve his prospects and try to make his way in the world.

At first he earned his living as a humble servant in a Welsh family in London, where he took his soundings and accustomed himself to the different pace of life in the capital. Next he showed considerable initiative by getting domestic employment in the family of Philip, the Earl of Pembroke, the Lord President of the Welsh Council. Having thus secured a firm, if humble foothold on the social ladder, he set about making himself so conspicuously useful that in time his prestigious master was pleased to take him into his personal service. When in 1625 Charles 1st came to the throne, John's master, the Earl of Pembroke was appointed to the royal household as the Lord Chamberlain in Whitehall, where before long, on the Earl's recommendation, John Henry too was taken into the King's service as the Keeper of the Orchard in Whitehall. At thirty-five years of age, his prospects were indeed fair. He had been provided with a house and a reasonable income; the young Welshman had arrived.

Before long John did what was expected of him and married, his choice falling on a London widow from nearby Westminster. She was to bear him six children, five daughters and a son, who was called Philip, in recognition of his family's obligation to the Earl of Pembroke, who was to become a most generous god-parent. It should be noted that this son was known as Philip Henry and not as Philip ap John, as Welsh custom formerly prescribed. Philip was born in 1631, a year after John's employer's first son was born, the future Charles II and two years before the King's second son was born, the future James II. Both the royal princes became the constant playmates of the young Philip, who all his life was to treasure a book which was given to him by the future James II.

John Henry's house was situated in the garden near the River Steps, where, in addition to his responsibilities as a gardener, he was also required to help all visitors, as they embarked or disembarked at the much-frequented River Steps. In the seventeenth century, when the river Thames was the main highway of London, the landing places were of considerable importance, none more so than these steps in the garden at Whitehall, which were to loom large in the life of the young Philip. William Laud, who in 1633 had become the Archbishop of Canterbury, frequently had to cross the river from his palace in Lambeth on his way to seeking audience with the King; in the course of these frequent journeys he became increasingly popular with John Henry and his son, who helped him ashore, with the result that, when misfortune befell the Archbishop and he was sent to the Tower of London, the King's Gardener and his young son sometimes visited him there. From these rather sombre visits they invariably returned home with gifts of money from the illustrious prisoner.

Philip in the 1630s seems to have had a full and happy childhood, enjoying excellent rapport with both of his parents. As to his education he first attended a school which was attached to St Martin-in-the-Fields, later moving to another school in Battersea. Meanwhile, he greatly enjoyed the companionship of the royal princes, while his mother saw to it that Philip accompanied her every Thursday when she went to a lecture at St Martin-in-the-Fields and again every Sunday when they attended even-song together at their parish church at St Margaret's Westminster. During these formative years Philip gave a general impression of being unusually studious in disposition.

External events however soon began to impinge upon the lives of them all; the clouds of political discord, which had been gathering ominously for some time between the King and his Parliament, led to the catastrophe of civil war in 1642. The very next year Philip Henry, now twelve years of age, was entered at Westminster School, transferring to the Upper School in 1646. Westminster School became for the youthful Philip a peaceful oasis in those troubled times, when his mother died as well as Archbishop Laud. His Headmaster, the famous Dr Busby came to think very highly of his Welsh pupil, regarding him as potentially an outstandingly able scholar. His Headmaster's high expectations were vindicated in 1647 when Philip Henry, aged 16, won a scholarship to Christ Church, Oxford; when he left school to take up this scholarship at Oxford, Philip received as a leaving present from his father's former employer, the Earl of Pembroke, a gift of £10, which Philip in his diary gratefully acknowledged to be a 'seasonable mercy'.

Going into residence at Oxford in October 1647, Philip was at once confronted with the need to answer a difficult question, on the answer to which his future career at the University depended. This indeed was the moment of decision; Parliament had won the civil war and had every intention of rooting out all supporters of the defeated Royalist cause. Hence at the beginning of term all members of the University, staff as well as students, were required to reply to the question: 'Will you submit to Parliament in the present visitation?' Philip's own tutor gave what was regarded by the authorities as an unsatisfactory reply and was in consequence forced to leave Oxford. Philip however managed to placate his interviewer by making the following tactful reply. 'I submit as far as I may with a safe conscience and without perjury.'

A year later, shortly before Christmas 1648, Philip qualified for a vacation in London, where he was able to stay for some weeks with his widowed father, who still lived near the Garden Steps in Whitehall. At the end of January 1649, while Philip was still at home, King Charles I was executed. Philip's diary described the scene. 'King Charles 1st went by our door on foot each day that he was carried to Whitehall, for he took the barge at Garden Steps, where we lived, and one day he spoke to my father. On the day of his execution, which was Tuesday, January 30th, I stood amongst the crowd in the street before Whitehall Gate, where the scaffold was erected, and saw what was done but was not near enough as to hear anything. The blow I saw given and can truly say with a sad heart; at the instant whereof there was such a groan as I never heard before and desire may never hear again.'

Back at Oxford after his traumatic vacation, Philip buckled down to work, graduating in 1652, the year in which his much-loved father died. The following year Philip was ordained in the Church of England and at once set about finding a suitable living. In view of what happened it is inevitable that some doubt should be felt about his sincerity in taking holy orders at this time; however Philip's private diary, which he certainly never intended any eyes but his own should see, gave no hint at all of any such doubts. Before long in 1653 he was offered the living of Worthenbury in Flintshire, which he gratefully accepted. The patron of the living was a judge who had recently received legal preferment as a reward for his services towards the victorious parliamentary cause. Furthermore his wife, Lady Puleston was a tireless and persuasive advocate of Parliament. Great changes were afoot at this time in church and state; the monarchy had gone and a republican commonwealth had taken its place with Oliver Cromwell the new master. In matters of religion local committees had been set up, which were authorised to appoint parish priests, which in a few years came to represent every possible shade of Protestant opinion.

At Worthenbury, Philip, more and more influenced by the view of Lady Puleston, became increasingly sympathetic to the Presbyterian outlook and in 1657 a seemingly anomalous situation arose when he, the Rector of Worthenbury, was also ordained a Presbyterian Minister at Prees, which was just over the national border in north Shropshire. This difficult position became well-nigh untenable when Lady Puleston and her husband, the Judge died in 1658 and 9; the new patron, the Judge's eldest son, Sir Roger Puleston was a staunch member of the Church of England, who in addition had been for a number of years at daggers drawn with Philip. All was not yet lost for Philip however because in 1660, the year in which the monarchy was restored in the person of Charles II, Philip decided to marry; no man ever made a better choice. Katherine was not only to become a loyal, devoted and utterly dependable wife. She also inherited a considerable fortune from her rich father which enabled her to help enormously in softening the economic blows that were to fall upon her husband in the following thirty years, when the firm stand he made for his Puritan principles often brought him into head-on collision with the law with the result that he often found himself in prison.

With the accession of Charles II in 1660, the religious experiments of the Commonwealth came to an abrupt end, with new legislation in the early 1660s giving all power back to the Church of England, to the total exclusion of all other ways of practising religion. In consequence Philip Henry was ejected from Worthenbury and thereafter preached his Puritanism whenever and wherever he could. His lot would then have been a very penurious one but for his wife's ability to use her money to maintain their growing family; eventually Philip and Katherine had six children. Their second son, Matthew, was born in 1662, he, who in the fulness of time became an outstanding nonconformist divine. At first Matthew was educated at home by a private tutor until at the age of eighteen in 1680 his father took him to London where he placed his son in a Dissenters' Academy, presided over by a Dr Doolittle. In 1685 Matthew, by then planning for a career in the law, enrolled at Gray's Inn, but a subsequent change of heart caused him in 1687 to be ordained as a dissident minister, who served successive ministries in Chester and in London, at Hackney.

In 1696 his father, Philip died and was buried in Whitchurch (Shropshire) in the parish church, where a wall-plaque commemorates his life. The old Puritan, though only sixty-five was worn out by the struggles of the years. The Welsh Biographical Dictionary has this to say. 'He left the impression of a man somewhat too scrupulous about cases of conscience but of his standard of life there can be no doubt he was a Christian gentleman of unimpeachable piety.' He fought the good fight, as did also his son Matthew, who in addition to being a devoted Minister was also a distinguished scholar who left as his memorial a Commentary on the Bible which has stood the test of time. Matthew died in 1714.

The seventeenth century produced many a diarist and it is just as well that Philip Henry was no exception, because, although Matthew wrote a book about his famous father, it is to the diary that one has to turn for an insight into the mind of this quite remarkable man. It was not until 1883 that these very revealing diaries were published. Historians are greatly indebted to a nineteenth century vicar, himself a descendant of Philip Henry, for collecting together these diaries and getting them published. His name was the Rev. Matthew Henry Lee. A far more famous seventeenth century diarist of course was Samuel Pepys; he, like Philip Henry, spent his boyhood in London, being educated at St Paul's School, while Philip went to Westminster. They both attended service at St Margaret's, Westminster and both witnessed the execution of Charles I, but as far as is known the two men never met.

In this seventeenth century family, there were indeed three generations of remarkable Welshmen, the grandfather, John, who became a servant and later the gardener of the King of

England, his son, Philip, scholar of Westminster and Christ Church, Oxford, who served as an Anglican priest before turning into a non-conformist rebel, and his son, Matthew, who switched from studying the law in London to become a non-conformist minister and an outstanding theological scholar. Could John ap Henry have known that morning, as he set out from Briton Ferry on his journey to London, what the fates had in store for those who were to come after him, he surely would have quickened his step.

COCHWILLAN
The 15th century house of a branch of the Penrhyn family
where John Williams was brought up.

Chapter 13

Two Welshmen at War

Until the 14th c. Welsh estates remained relatively small, thanks to the operation of gavelkind, a law of inheritance which insisted that a man's property at death should be divided between his sons; thereafter however there was a gradual though general switch from gavelkind to primogeniture, which allowed the eldest son to inherit the estate. This significant change enabled a new social class to emerge in Wales, the gentry, whose power base was the land. By the 17th c. this social change had acquired political momentum, which was to become obvious when the new Welsh gentry took the side of the King in his struggle with Parliament in the Civil War.

Such was the social background of John Williams. On his father's side he was descended from a younger branch of the Gruffydd family of Penrhyn; their 15th c. house at Cochwillan, near Llanllechid, east of the A5 between Llandygái and Bethesda, has miraculously managed at least vestigially to have survived. His mother's forebears were none other than the Wynns, whose mansion at Gwydir, near Llanrwst in the Conwy Valley, was likewise built in the 15th c.

Such too was the social background of another Welshman, John Owen, who, like John Williams, was born with a silver spoon in his mouth. John Owen hailed from the remote and beautiful Pennant Valley, west of Snowdon, his family home, Clenennau, lying between Dolbenmaen and Penmorfa. His father had been secretary to Elizabeth's great Secretary of State, the mysterious Sir Francis Walsingham. John Owen too was born into the gentry and he too became involved in the Civil War on the King's side. These two men, John Williams and John Owen, both of outstanding calibre, despite throwing in their lot with the King, yet were to fight a private war, one with the other. After the lapse of more than 350 years it should be possible to view the clash dispassionately, while still registering dismay that such a clash ever took place.

John Williams was born in Conwy in March 1582, the second son of Edmund and Mary Williams, his illustrious grandfather being Sir John Wynn himself. All his life John Williams regarded himself first and foremost as a son of Conwy, within whose historic walls so many momentous events in his later life took place. He was educated at Ruthin Grammar School before going up to Cambridge in 1598. After graduating in theology, John Williams was duly ordained and prepared himself for a successful career in the church, to which his qualifications, his background and his affluence clearly pointed, even though there was little enough evidence of any spiritual involvement. Meanwhile storm clouds were beginning to gather in the world outside, as a conflict started to take shape between the King and Parliament, between those who favoured a despotic monarchy and those who preferred the sovereignty to belong to Parliament. James Ist came to rely more and more upon the advice given him by extra-parliamentary aristocrats, of whom far the most influential was the future Duke of Buckingham, who was also to become the close friend and confidant of the future Charles I.

In 1612 the Lord Chancellor of England, acting on the advice of James Ist, before whom John Williams had preached the previous year, made the rising Welshman his personal chaplain, in which office the theological scholar soon showed a clear intention of becoming an enthusiastic politician. Buckingham too approved of Williams, who in 1619 took another giant step up the ecclesiastical ladder, when he became Dean of Salisbury. To this honour was added the following year the even more lucrative and prestigious preferment to the deanery of Westminster. The climax was reached in 1621 when James I, thanks partly to the advice of Buckingham and partly to the reliance the King placed on Williams' ability to give sound advice, appointed him Lord Keeper of the Seal and at the same time made him Bishop of Lincoln. John Williams was not yet thirty-nine.

While John Williams was making such startling progress in church and state, John Owen, who had been born in 1600 and was thus eighteen years younger than John Williams, was beginning to make his mark in Welsh affairs. Having succeeded to the family estates in 1626, four years later he became Sheriff of Caernarfon, when only thirty years of age; the next year he also became Sheriff of Meirionnydd. Friends of the King will have noted his increasingly powerful position in Gwynedd so that, when hostilities broke out in 1642, the King ordered John Owen to raise and train an army, to be drawn from the three counties of Gwynedd, – Anglesey, Meirionnydd and Caernarfon.

The careers of these two future rivals took very different directions in the years before the war broke out in 1642, with John Owen steadily strengthening his already strong position in Gwynedd, while the career of John Williams, in the upper echelons of government, suffered a very severe setback, which, with the benefit of hindsight, must have seemed likely once Charles I succeeded his father in 1625. Charles' chief adviser was Buckingham who became the firm ally of the up and coming leader of the Church of England, William Laud, both of whom stoutly backed the royal assertion of the Divine Right of Kings. All this happened at a time when the Keeper of the Royal Seal, the virtual Head of Government, in the person of John Williams, again and again advised his royal master to avoid a confrontation with Parliament. The King ignored this advice and dismissed him from his high office. The latter quietly withdrew from public life for the time being and devoted himself to his bishopric in Lincoln, where he stayed until 1637.

The King from 1629 to 1640 chose to rule the country without once summoning a parliament; in these years of arbitrary royal rule the position of William Laud became ever stronger, especially after 1633 when the King made him Archbishop of Canterbury. Thus strengthened, Laud gathered together evidence, real or false, of John Williams' illegal acts, while Keeper of the Royal Seal, citing the alleged betrayal of state secrets and perjury. Finally in 1637 John Williams was arrested and brought before the infamous Court of Star Chamber in London. The outcome was a fine of £10,000, suspension from the See of Lincoln and imprisonment in the Tower of London, where he had to languish until 1640.

Late in 1640 the King, reduced to desperately straitened circumstances by lack of money, had to swallow his pride and summon parliament, which at once ordered the release of John Williams from the Tower. The main objective of this parliament, later to be known as the Long Parliament, was to get the legal relationship of the King to Parliament clearly defined and for ever enshrined in statute. To make their task the easier Parliament first ordered the arrest of Laud; the King, thus bereft of his normal source of support, decided, in an attempt to win over public opinion, to summon John Williams to advise him once more. By the end of 1641 his fortunes seemed about to be restored to their former heights, when the King made him Archbishop of York. By this preferment Williams was now virtually Head of the Church of England, as Laud, the Archbishop of Canterbury, was never to leave the Tower except to be executed.

In June 1642 Williams went to York where he was consecrated. Two months later the Royal Standard was raised in Nottingham and the Civil War had begun. When John Williams learnt that a party of Parliamentary soldiers was approaching his palace, he fled from York and sought the security of the walls of Conwy Castle, which he soon left for a brief visit to Oxford where he pledged his loyalty to the King before returning to Conwy where he set about attending to the needs of the town and castle. At his own expense he greatly improved the fortifications of the castle, he laid in supplies and he strengthened the garrison. Meanwhile he kept in constant touch with the King, being Charles' chief and most valuable source of information on developments in north Wales and more particularly in Ireland, where a full-blooded rebellion had broken out in 1641. Ormonde had been despatched to Ireland by the King to try to contain the outbreak, taking with him an army, in the ranks of which were many Welshmen. By 1643 the Irish rebellion seemed to have quietened down sufficiently for Ormonde to agree to the King's request to send home the Welsh contingent. John Williams made detailed arrangements for the eventual reception of the Welsh soldiers both in Beaumaris and in Conwy, where the returning soldiers were to be fed, re-clothed and rearmed for further service in the royal cause nearer home. By the end of 1643 John Williams was ready for anything, but he still awaited the arrival of the Welsh soldiers, whose return in fact Ormonde was never to authorise. At any rate Conwy Castle was equipped for all eventualities, prompting Williams before the year was out to ask his royal master to make him its Governor.

John Owen, meanwhile, having duly raised and armed an army in Gwynedd, as the King had ordered, marched at its head into England; he took part in an engagement outside Oxford in May 1643, then in July he commanded a brigade under Prince Rupert at the siege of Bristol, where he was wounded, recovering in time to participate in further fighting at Newbury in September. It was not until April 1646 that Owen was back in Caernarfon, where the King promptly made him Sheriff again. From that moment John Williams had a rival on the spot; in December of the same year Williams learnt to his chagrin that the Governorship of Conwy to which he had aspired had been given to John Owen, together with a knighthood. Spurned as he felt himself to have been, John Williams stayed on in Conwy Castle as the 'de facto' Governor until the Spring of 1645 when Sir John Owen forcibly but, of course, legally expelled the Archbishop, who for the time being withdrew to Bangor.

This local quarrel, humiliating as it was for John Williams, was of little consequence compared with the grave decline in the Royalist fortunes not many miles away in Chester, to which important base a parliamentary army laid siege in the early summer of 1645. Throughout this fatal year for the King's cause Charles pleaded all in vain for reinforcement to be sent from Ireland; in a forlorn attempt to relieve the siege Charles led an army against the parliamentary forces that were encamped outside the city walls. The resulting battle at Rowton Moor, outside Chester, in September was disastrous for the King. The city of Chester was to hold out for a few more months but finally surrendered to Parliament in May 1646.

With the fall of Chester the first Civil War virtually came to an end because Charles, feeling at the end of his tether, when his own headquarters at Oxford were shortly afterwards besieged, managed to slip out and surrendered to the Scottish army, which by that time had come as far south as Newark and become the allies of Parliament. John Williams, faced by a new situation after Chester's fall, in the early summer of 1646 wrote a tactful letter to Sir John Owen, hoping that thereby the breach between them might somehow be healed, but receiving only an uncompromising reply, made contact with Mytton, the Parliamentary general, who was in the process of systematically reducing those coastal towns in north Wales that had sided with the King. In this connection it is interesting to learn that Williams' letter to Mytton drew a reply from none other than Oliver Cromwell, who had been baptised Williams. In his letter Cromwell, while accepting John Williams' offer to help, acknowledged himself to be the archbishop's cousin.

In the Autumn Mytton's forces, now unexpectedly aided and abetted by Williams and his men, captured the town of Conwy and in November the castle too, its defender Sir John Owen being allowed to leave and return to his home in the Pennant Valley on certain stringent conditions. John Williams' defection however was no isolated affair as many of the gentry in north Wales, feeling that the war had been lost and that ordinary men and women in north Wales had suffered enough, also decided to throw in their lot with the parliamentary forces and so help to bring to a speedy conclusion a sorry chapter in the history of north Wales.

After the Parliamentary capture of Conwy John Williams went to live at Cloddaeth Hall, which still stands across the water from Conwy, a mile or two behind Deganwy. In 1648, Prince Rupert, ready to take up arms again the Royal cause, appealed to Sir John Owen to defy authority and to raise another army in Merioneth. This he did, but in June of that same year he was ambushed near Bangor and was taken to London to be tried for treason. Charles I was executed at the end of January 1649 and little more than a month later John Owen was also sentenced to death for treason. He appealed against the sentence and to the surprise of most people he was freed, hearsay insisting that he was reprieved through the personal intervention of Oliver Cromwell. Whatever the reason for this quite unexpected development, he was once more allowed to go back home to Clenennau, but this time under virtual house arrest.

News of the death of Charles I reached John Williams, when he was staying at Gwydir Castle with his kinsmen, where, some think, he came to regret his defection from the royal cause. In March 1650 he died at home at Cloddaeth and was buried at Llandygái, where a monument on the church wall, along with his helmet and spurs, serves to commemorate him. He was a scholar, a statesman, a church leader and in his old age a man of action; John Williams was a true son of the Renaissance and one of the greatest Welshmen of his age. In a quieter century he would have been able to devote more of his time to his undoubted love of fine arts, music and architecture. The Archbishop was certainly an opportunist but also a man of wise moderation, whose counsels, had they been heeded, might well have guided the storm-tossed ship of state into calmer waters.

Sir John Owen for his part lived quietly and unobtrusively at Clenennau through the tumultuous times of the

Commonwealth until August 1659, when, sensing a change in the air, the old warrior once again put on his spurs and joined a well-timed rebellion, which in the early summer of 1660 succeeded in putting Charles II on the throne. As reward for serving the royal cause so well he received the title of Vice-Admiral of North Wales. Six years later he died in Clenennau; he was an uncomplicated man who lacked all political skill and guile. He was a soldier first and last, who against all the odds died in his own bed.

THE FIELD PULPIT AT TREFECA
Two hundred years ago this field pulpit, which occupies a prominent position in the museum at Trefeca today, was called into use on very special occasions. Among those who preached from it, over and apart from Howell Harris himself, were Daniel Rowland, William Williams and John Wesley. Augustus Toplady, who had himself preached there, wrote that on one occasion 'no fewer than one thousand, three hundred horses were turned into one large field near the college . . . the carriages were also unusually numerous'. Many years later it was discovered in a smithy at Bronllys; it was brought back to Trefeca in the 1920's.

Chapter 14

The Family at Trefeca

About 1700 a joiner, Harris by name, in search of employment, moved from Carmarthenshire to the Talgarth area, north-east of Brecon, where two years later he married a local girl, Susannah of Trefeca, a village south of Talgarth. Of the five children of the marriage, three were boys, of whom the youngest was born in 1714 and christened Howell. In his formative years Howell was something of a lay-about until on Palm Sunday, 1735, when he was twenty-one, he was so overcome by a sermon preached in Talgarth's parish church, which called sinners to repentance, that his whole life was changed. Thereafter he devoted himself to changing the lives of others, as he sought ordination to the Church of England from his Bishop. He went about button-holing his former layabout friends, he preached at street corners, he did all he could in a highly emotional way to make people mend their ways. The Church of England was unimpressed, and the Bishop, who was applied to by Harris four times, unequivocally refused to consider him suitable for ordination.

The die was cast; everyone expected Howell to join the ranks of the Dissenters, but this he steadfastly refused to do, although thousands flocked to hear him preach outdoors, thus presenting him with the problem of keeping in touch with the many whom he had converted. This he managed to do by organising them into little local groups, which he called Societies. The early meetings of these Societies constituted the first beginning of what was to become the Methodist Movement in Wales. In 1737 on one of his preaching tours he met a fellow-Christian, Daniel Rowland who was already a curate with the Church of England; this meeting was of the utmost importance for the religious reform movement in Wales, because its ultimate success rested on the shoulders of these two gifted men, helped by a third, William Williams, of Pantycelyn, who became Wales' outstanding hymn-writer.

From 1738 the Methodist Movement in Wales gained substantial momentum as the partnership of the two young enthusiasts began to develop and to bear fruit. So successful did the Movement become that its members clamoured for a leader to be chosen. Meanwhile Howell Harris had married; his wife, Anne Williams, a simple Radnorshire girl, was to provide a haven of protection for her headstrong and rather over-powering husband. Howell was temperamentally unsuited to be second to anyone – he had a truly remarkable skill at planning and organising, while his rival, Daniel Rowland was an impassioned orator, who frequently moved his congregations to tears. By 1750 the Methodist Movement in Wales had chosen Rowland, and William Williams agreed with their choice: Howell Harris felt himself to be alone, deserted, thwarted and misunderstood by his friends; physically he was near a breakdown but his extraordinary mental energy drove him into entering upon a course of action, for which he deserves to be long remembered, a course of action, of which the seeds had been sown some years before in London, when he had first met John Wesley.

A few years previously John Wesley had returned from a visit to America, where his path had crossed that of some Moravian missionaries, who had fired him with enthusiasm, which he was to communicate to his friends back in London, one of whom was Howell Harris. Wherever Moravians settled, they tended to form communities, which, though fundamentally of a religious nature, were also social and economic groups in so far as they encouraged all their members to ply their trades in these communities. Harris had this socio-religious experiment of the Moravians very much in mind, when he started out to organise what became known as his Family in Trefeca in 1752.

That he was able in the Spring of that year to attempt this Herculean task of demolition and building was above all due to the munificence of Madame Griffith, with whom Howell had enjoyed a bizarre relationship since 1746, when she came to one of his meetings in north Wales. Thereafter she fastened on to him like a leech, frequently staying in Trefeca with Howell and his wife. Her sudden death in 1752 made it possible for him to start the building programme, as Madame Griffith had left him £900 with an express injunction that the money was to be spent on the building. First he had his old home demolished before setting about the erection of the first of the Family's buildings, which was a large house with seven rooms on the ground floor, another seven rooms above with three attic bedrooms on top. Here the very first members of the Family lived. By the following year the number of residents had increased to twenty-nine, of whom twenty-eight came from Wales, fourteen from north Wales and fourteen from the south and one from Shropshire. Further buildings appeared as new needs arose, until when John Wesley visited the Family he found what he called a little paradise where one hundred and twenty people lived and worked and worshipped God. Whatever its appearance (William Williams called it 'a castellated monastery') – and there was no doubt that the buildings constituted in its heyday a substantial settlement – what really mattered was that a full viable communal life was set in motion to which all members of the Family made their separate contributions in labour and in worship. On arrival new members handed over all their money to the Family treasury, where it was scrupulously looked after. On one occasion, for instance, when a young woman, after a short while, left the Family to marry outside the settlement, she found her money waiting for her.

At Trefeca full scope was given to the founder's genius for organising, as from small beginnings no fewer than sixty trades and crafts were practised. The very extensive grounds were laid out with gardens, orchards and fish ponds, as well as into fields, where crops were grown and animals raised. Flax was an important crop as there was a thriving and essential shirt-making craft, while the wool from the backs of the home-produced sheep provided the wherewithal for the manufacture of blankets. Cattle and pigs were also reared, while joinery and building were necessary trades, successfully practised at Trefeca. Harris himself developed a special interest in agriculture and in 1755 became one of the original members of the Brecknockshire Agricultural Society which was the first in Wales. There were in addition on the staff a matron, who was responsible for the welfare of the women and the children and the sick, and a business manager, whose task it was to find satisfactory markets for the products of the Family's fields and workshops. As well as the in-workers of the community, who comprised the core of the Family, there were many other adherents who lived in rented farms in the district, where in addition to growing food for the Family they were allowed to participate in the religious life of the community.

If the thorough organisation of the daily work was absolutely essential for the continued well-being and indeed for the very existence of the community, Howell Harris never let it be forgotten that the underlying purpose of every moment of the Family's life was the worship of God. Harris believed in his heart that not only God had to be remembered in acts of work and worship and in every conscious thought, but, believing that Satan finds work for idle hands to do, he saw to it that unorganised leisure had no place in life at Trefeca. Every work-day was very rigorous. Breakfast at four o'clock in the morning was followed by a sermon, given by one of a panel of four chosen speakers; all this was before work began at six in the morning, work which went on until the midday meal at one p.m., after which Harris briefly addressed the assembled workers before they returned to field and bench. The day's toil ended between seven and eight in the evening; half an hour later Harris delivered his daily lecture before the evening meal was taken at nine p.m. Bed and lights-out followed at ten o'clock. On Sunday the Family went to church and took Holy Communion.

The success of the Family experiment greatly benefited

Harris' health so that by the middle 1750s he was restored to his former good spirits, as his physical strength returned. Gradually too, to this infinite satisfaction, he managed to win over his wife to a full appreciation of the value of the community. It appears that Harris devoted all his mornings to religious exercises, reading, praying and meditation, and, of course, to preparing the daily lecture, while in the afternoons he supervised and inspected the work of the various activities. In addition he spent what time and energy he could spare on the affairs of the Brecknockshire Agricultural Society. In 1756 he felt strong enough in mind and body to resume preaching away from Trefeca. The settlement had prospered so well in terms of material profit that in 1758 a printing press was bought, which did much subsequently to make known the achievements of the Family. By 1759 Harris felt that the settlement was well-enough established for him to absent himself for a period, which circumstances caused to be extended to three years.

The war that had broken out between the United Kingdom and France in 1756, which historians call the Seven Years' War, and which represented the next phase in a colonial struggle between the two countries, was seen by Harris as a struggle between Protestants and Roman Catholics, so that, when three years later there seemed a distinct likelihood that the forces of Roman Catholic France might attempt an invasion of the Protestant United Kingdom, he felt himself personally involved. It must be remembered that when the war had begun three years previously he had persuaded five young men in the Family to volunteer for the Army, three of whom were with General Wolfe at the siege of Quebec. In 1759 Howell Harris with another twenty-four members of the Family joined the Militia, but before he actually donned the King's uniform, he asked and received permission, while on Active Service, to preach, whenever the opportunity arose. This strange military interlude came to an end when he was demobilised in Brecon in December 1762, enabling him once again to preside over the Family at Christmas that year.

When leading Methodists in Wales heard that Harris was leaving the Army they wrote him a letter, which a great many signed, welcoming him back to Wales and expressing the fervent hope that old quarrels would be patched up. Seeing that two of the signatories were Daniel Rowland and William Williams the outlook for unity in the Methodist Movement became distinctly brighter.

Meanwhile the Family continued to function at Trefeca as a thriving community. So well had Harris laid the foundations in the early 1750s that it seemed to withstand easily the strain of his three years of absence. For the remaining eleven years of his life, while keeping an attentive eye on the life of the community, he felt free to resume much of his earlier work away from home. A year of outstanding activity was 1769, when for a while the fervent vigour of his youth seemed briefly to return. Much happened in that year to give him satisfaction, including the visit to Trefeca of John Wesley, George Whitefield, Daniel Rowland and William Williams. In March 1770, however, the shadows lengthened with the death of his wife, Anne. The grief of that separation, along with his own declining health hit him very hard. From then on he stayed at Trefeca with the Family. In his last years he was much comforted by a ripening friendship with the Vicar of Talgarth. The end came in 1773, a few months before his sixtieth birthday. He died as he lived, a member of the Church of England and he was buried inside the parish church at Talgarth, his funeral causing the biggest crowd ever known to assemble in the streets of the little Brecknockshire town.

After the death of Howell Harris, the Family decided to carry on and indeed struggled manfully into the nineteenth century, though as the stream of new members began to dry up, the various trades dwindled away. The Family virtually ceased to exist in 1820, nine years after Welsh Methodists had finally broken away from the Church of England and become the Welsh Calvinist Methodist Church. The highly important Trefeca Press continued to publish until 1806, their most memorable book possibly being the Life of Howell Harris, which was published in 1791.

Religious activity continued to flourish at Trefeca. In 1838 the two surviving trustees of the Family handed the property over to the Brecknockshire Monthly Meeting, which in turn offered it to the Calvinist Methodist Church in south Wales. At Trefeca in 1842 a training college for Calvinist Methodist ministers was opened, which continued until 1906, when it became an inter-denominational theological college. This college ceased to function in 1964, but the buildings were called back into use in 1966 as a Residential Centre. The college today is a lay training centre for the Presbyterian Church of Wales (the Calvinist Methodists). Parts of the original buildings were pulled down in 1872 and on the site was erected the Howell Harris Memorial Chapel, adjoining which is the Howell Harris Museum, a visit to which is recommended to all those who for religious or historical reasons find the study of the second half of the eighteenth century in this part of Wales an absorbing one. In a different setting, in a well-populated area this display of eighteenth century exhibits associated with Howell Harris and the Family would excite considerable interest. As it is, to the discriminating a visit to Trefeca today, both outdoors and to the Museum, is a wholly delightful voyage of discovery.

LLANCARFAN CHURCH

The village of Llancarfan near which Edward Williams, also known as Iolo Morganwg, was born, is an ancient place whose history dates back to the 6th c., when one of St Illtud's contemporaries, St Cadoc built a monastery there which came to rival even St Illtud's great seminary at Llanilltud (Llantwit). The church, here illustrated, is thought to stand on the site of St Cadoc's monastic buildings.

Iolo's family later moved further west to Flemingston, to which place in the Vale of Glamorgan he chose to return to spend his unhappy retirement years. He died there and was buried in the churchyard nearby, which is less than two miles west of Llancarfan, as the crow flies, though considerably further on foot, thanks to the intervening Thaw valley.

Chapter 15

An Eighteenth Century Sabbatical Year

It needs to be said at once that the phrase 'Sabbatical Year', used in the title of this chapter, refers to its modern rather than to its ancient usage, by which, according to the Book of Exodus, in the Old Testament, Jews were required to let their land lie fallow every seventh year. In modern times, however, the practice has grown for certain fortunate and successful academics occasionally to be granted a year's absence from their posts, nominally in order to further their researches into their chosen fields of study, in the course of which, if credence is to be given to popular belief, academic batteries are sometimes recharged in unusual and agreeable ways! That readers may be able to savour to the full this unusual eighteenth century sabbatical year it is first necessary to put them in possession of sundry relevant biographical details from the early life of Edward Williams, who as a result of his mid-life change of occupation and residence saw fit thereafter to change his name to Iolo Morganwg.

Edward Williams was born in 1747 in a small cottage near Llancarfan in the Vale of Glamorgan, where his father had set up as a stone mason. In the early 1750s the family moved to Flemingston, a village three miles south-east of Cowbridge, to which place he returned in his declining years to spend his unhappy, impoverished last days. Though as a boy he was trained by his father to follow in his footsteps as a stone mason, it was to his mother that he looked as his guiding light. Anne Williams was a proud and well-read woman, who taught her son to read. At nine years of age Edward started his life's work as a stone mason but in the evenings he sat in front of the fire listening to his mother as she either read to him or more often told him stories of the great figures in Glamorgan's past history. Although there was no school for him to attend, he received a sympathetic education from his mother, who taught him to read English before introducing him to his native literature. Three things she took particular pleasure in imparting to her attentive audience, a knowledge of books, a love of music, and, most important of all, the past history of the great families who had in former centuries brought fame to her beloved Glamorgan. Edward above all was to cherish the cultural heritage of his own county, a love which his mother first inculcated in him; once in possession of this strong love, he was next taught to read Welsh books. If one thing mattered more to him in later life than Glamorgan, it was the Welsh language, which became the love of his life. Scholars who are familiar with his writings in both languages have no doubt at all that it was as a writer in Welsh rather than in English that he truly excelled. While still in Flemingston he seems also to have enjoyed the company of a number of young fellow craftsmen, who shared his interest in poetry, in religious dissent and in thinking what his seniors were later to regard as dangerous political thoughts.

In 1770, when Edward was 23, he left Glamorgan for London, which in the second half of the eighteenth century proved to be a magnet to young Welshmen, who gathered there in search of fame and fortune. So many of them were there that they formed associations, of which the best known was the Honourable Society of Cymmrodorion of which Edward was fortunate enough to become a member. There he met Welshmen who encouraged him in his literary endeavours. First however he had to establish himself as a stone mason, which trade in time provided him with the necessary money and leisure to enable him to devote his spare time to furthering his growing reputation as a writer. This first stay in London lasted until 1777; in these formative years he wrote a great deal and often had pieces published both in Welsh and English periodicals.

Edward Williams was always a great walker so that when he walked home from London in 1777 it was hardly surprising that he made a détour through Bristol, visiting on the way Avebury and Stonehenge, which greatly excited him. The picture coming down to us is of a sturdy figure, carrying a stick as tall as himself, with his spectacles well down his nose. He once walked from Oxford to London (fifty-four miles), while on another occasion he trudged from Flemingston to Bristol (forty-seven miles), conducted his business, spent the night in a friend's armchair and next morning walked back home, having covered ninety-four miles inside two days, with but four meals to sustain him, all consisting of his favourite food, slices of bread and butter, washed down with a great many cups of sweet milky tea. He was practically a vegetarian and he rarely touched alcohol. He maintained that there were three things for which he had no need, a horse, because he had a good pair of legs, a cellar, because he never drank beer, and a purse, because he could never keep money. No one who knew him could possibly doubt the truth of this third claim, least of all his future wife, who was to suffer acutely from his prodigality with her money.

On this long peripatetic walk back home from London, he will have had ample opportunities for reflecting on the momentous events that were beginning to unfold in the American colonies, where the previous year on the 4th of July 1776 the colonists had declared their independence from the mother country. Edward Williams, who was by nature a rebel, with an inborn dislike of the Establishment, cannot but have been encouraged and excited by transatlantic developments, which he will have fervently hoped would be imitated in Europe, particularly in France, where all the seeds of revolution were germinating fast.

Back in Flemingston, Edward, reunited with his patient, long-suffering father looked around for suitable employment, without having recourse to his own trade of stone mason, which had apparently done damage to his lungs. At the same time he renewed his courtship of Margaret Roberts, which he had allowed to lapse. Her home was only a mile or so from Flemingston. Suffice it to say that the marriage finally took place in 1781, a year that was memorable for the abject surrender of the British army at Yorktown, which presaged the almost certain military defeat of Britain by the Americans. Back to Flemingston, where Margaret Roberts was to show herself to be a very doughty character indeed; in the years ahead again and again she revealed quite astonishing qualities of toughness and durability, which somehow enabled her to stay with her more than difficult husband. Moreover she was intelligent and well-read – and in possession of a considerable amount of money, which was to pass through her husband's fingers with almost unbelievable rapidity.

The next year 1782 must have uplifted Edward's spirits; his first child, Peggy was born, the Government in London recognised the independence of the American colonies and a man of Glamorgan, a nonconformist minister, David Williams, published his Letters of Political Liberty, a book which was to find much favour with republican would-be revolutionaries in France. David Williams was soon invited to Paris, where he was consulted by Robespierre; Edward at once became an admirer of his revolutionary ideas and soon became closely associated with this other Glamorgan Williams.

Meanwhile Edward took full advantage of his wife's money to try his hand at various ways of earning his living, twice in 1783 setting himself up as a builder, once in Llandaf and once in Cardiff. Both ventures failing, Margaret then provided the capital for him to buy a coastal vessel in which he hoped to trade between Bristol and the ports in south Wales. Finally all Margaret's money having been spent in vain, Edward, Margaret and the infant Peggy in 1785 fled by night to Wells in Somerset, to escape the clutches of their many creditors, who soon closed in on them, forcing them to flee, once again by night and back to Flemingston, where the law caught up with them. Edward Williams was arrested, brought to trial and sent to prison for a year. Here in Cardiff's prison for debtors Edward was to stay from 1786 to 1787; here he was to spend his sabbatical year.

Few men can ever have enjoyed a sabbatical year so much or derived so much benefit from one. The powers that be certainly did the prisoner proud; for a whole year he was provided with board and accommodation and the leisure to pursue his many and varied interests. Here Edward celebrated his fortieth birthday, his friends and family gathering together to mark the occasion. His father, most generous and long-suffering of men, visited him frequently and provided him with all necessary creature comforts, while he also financed the removal of Edward's wife and child to a house in a street near the gaol. Edward grasped with both hands this unique and unexpected opportunity to sit and think, to look backward and to survey the future. He was allowed to correspond at great length with many whose ideas and interests matched his own; he read widely, he thought deeply and held what can only be called seminars in prison – and still found time to learn to play the flute. Above all, he reached new heights in achievement in his own writing, both of poetry and prose.

There is however a darker side to report; he developed in Cardiff prison a real talent for forgery. Thanks to his previous research in London and elsewhere into the work of Wales' greatest medieval poet, Dafydd ap Gwilym, he knew a very great deal about him. Armed with this knowledge, he proceeded to write in prison many poems, in which he imitated quite brilliantly the great poet's style. A harmless, scholarly pastime, it might be thought but for the fact that he announced to the world, when he had these poems published in a book, to which he wrote a foreword, that he had discovered these masterpieces by Dafydd ap Gwilym in remote and unspecified parts of Glamorgan for which county he hoped thereby greatly to increase its cultural heritage. To cap this mid-life break from reality and responsibility, while still in prison, his wife gave birth to a second child, a boy, Taliesin, who eventually became his father's literary executor.

He emerged from prison an even fiercer radical, ready for action; he was on the crest of a wave, a new man with a new name, the success of his book on Dafydd ap Gwilym deciding him to change his name to Iolo Morganwg (Edward of Glamorgan). Back home with wife and children, he set about discovering or inventing evidence of Druidism in past centuries in Glamorgan. Readers are here recommended to look ahead to Chapter 20 where Iolo's activities on behalf of Druidism merged into a resurgence of the eisteddfod movement at the end of the eighteenth and the beginning of the nineteenth centuries. Meanwhile, back in Flemingston Iolo was becoming restless, the novelty of freedom having worn off. When in 1789 word reached him of the meeting of the Estates-General in Paris, which was to herald the start of the French Revolution, he made his plans and in 1791, regardless of family needs and his responsibilities, set out again for London, where he found that his reputation had grown apace since he left the capital fourteen years before.

In the same month, September 1792, in which Iolo was to hold his Gorsedd on Primrose Hill, the cold-blooded murder of many Royalists in France produced a profound shock in London. These events caused critical glances to fall upon known sympathisers, such as Iolo, whose London home was raided and his papers seized. He was ordered to report to Whitehall for an interview, which was conducted by Pitt himself, who, to Iolo's great relief, appeared satisfied. Meanwhile his literary reputation continued to grow in London, hastened by his latest publication which received very favourable comment from many, notably William Wilberforce and George Washington.

It was at this juncture, in 1795, with his London reputation at its peak, that his neglect of his family caught up with him. The death of his father a few months previously had deprived Iolo's wife and children of their only source of maintenance. Iolo returned to find a state of utter destitution. Somehow a move to Cowbridge was arranged where Iolo began to find work once more as a stone mason but the state of his lungs soon put a stop to this experiment. Thereafter the family had to depend upon the charity and kindness, especially of London friends, to keep the wolf from the door until Iolo managed to find profitable employment in the Board of Agriculture, who authorised him to report to them upon the state of agriculture in certain parts of south Wales.

In February 1797 came news of the abortive French landing in west Pembrokeshire; local republican feelings died overnight. Even Iolo was moved to write a recruiting song for the Glamorgan Volunteers. He was now fifty and in poor health; he stayed in Wales for the rest of his life, concentrating his interest on Druidism and Unitarianism. He particularly stressed two aspects of Druidism, nature worship and a belief in one god. Soon he became a Unitarian and saw no inconsistency in embracing both faiths.

Before long a rapid decline in health made it necessary for Iolo to go back to his old home in Flemingston, where his devoted daughter, Peggy, already looked after her blind mother. Here Iolo spent his last remaining years, becoming less and less tolerant of every attempt to interfere with his crazy life style, which no sensible daughter could have been expected to countenance. Sometimes he wrote all through the night, keeping himself awake with innumerable cups of tea and becoming more and more dependent on the pain-killing properties of laudanum. The end came suddenly just before Christmas in 1826, less than three weeks before his eightieth birthday. He was buried in the churchyard at Flemingston, quite close to his cottage.

It is not easy to make a proper appraisal of this undoubtedly remarkable man. He was a great Welsh scholar, poet and prose writer, despite all the forgeries, probably prompted by his overzealous attachment to Glamorgan. That he was one of the main influences in modern Welsh culture cannot be gainsaid. He was also the father of Welsh nationalism and he turned the eisteddfod into a great national institution.

*This statue of Dr William Price was erected
to his memory in 1982 amid scenes of great enthusiasm.
It stands in the Bull Ring at Llantrisant.*

Chapter 16

The Legalising of Cremation

Every now and again Nature produces a sport; gardeners are familiar with the excitement caused by the appearance of the occasional freak. In the year 1800 such a sport appeared in a valley in south Wales, a few miles north-west of Cardiff, where in the house of the Rev. Price and his wife a baby was born, christened William, the youngest of seven children. His parentage was unusual, his father a former classical scholar at Oxford, and later a Fellow of Jesus College, his mother dim-witted and completely illiterate. William's father, having taught him until he was ten, at fourteen apprenticed him to a surgeon in Pontypridd from whom he later went to St Bartholomew's Hospital in London, from where he emerged as a brilliant young surgeon, who at 21, well-equipped professionally, returned to Wales to practise what he had learned among the coal miners in Pontypridd and district.

There he soon acquired a reputation for being a clever and caring doctor, but of eccentric habits; for instance, he always wore a white smock with a red jersey over it and his trousers were invariably green and over his head he wore the skin of a fox, whose brush dangled down his back. To complete the picture he also sported a long black beard. In the twenties and thirties his fame as an eccentric greatly increased; he never accepted payment, if he failed to cure his patient, and he insisted on paying all his visits at night, while he utterly refused to treat any patient who smoked.

Like Iolo Morganwg before him, he took an abiding interest in Druidism, an interest which in the depressed social conditions of the 1830s, when conditions in the mines were appalling and the wages minimal, had to give way to Chartism, on behalf of which Dr Price also continuously agitated. Although he played no active part in the abortive Chartist march on Newport in 1839, his name was on the Wanted listed and he had to flee to France, where he stayed until the trouble blew over.

Once back in Wales however, he busied himself again with his practice, where his patients more than ever looked for him for help in their social distress. With all his eccentric ways and his repeated flouting of the law, Dr Price was a man with a social conscience; he was a true friend of the underprivileged. His ability to stand up for himself in a court of law was well illustrated in 1873, when he defended himself successfully against a charge of professional incompetence. The dice seemed loaded against him when he played his trump card and demanded the services of another doctor to conduct a post-mortem, which in the event completely exonerated him.

William Price, on the occasion of this legal victory, was seventy three years of age; his reputation as a doctor stood very high in Llantrisant where he then practised. Most doctors in his position would have looked back on a career of some professional achievement, along with a few ups and downs, and would have decided rather belatedly that the time had come for them to slacken off into retirement. Not so Dr Price; his greatest adventure still lay ahead of him, an adventure which was to make his name familiar to a wider audience and which would assure him of a place in history, as the man who, despite enormous opposition, was responsible for getting cremation accepted as a legal alternative to burial.

In the ancient world cremation was commonly practised but on the advent of Christianity it was forbidden in the West, where Christians came to believe in the physical resurrection of the body, which cremation was assumed to rule out. Over the centuries, however, in western Europe, churchyards became overcrowded; first the unconsecrated northern sides of the churchyards were consecrated and called into use as burial grounds, but the problem of overcrowding was again to recur when, in the fullness of time, with the growth of population, even the north sides were often used up. Periodically the church authorities sanctioned the removal of bones from early graves to charnel houses, which came to be regarded as half-way houses to bone-fires in the churchyard the following All Hallow E'en. In the nineteenth century there was a very rapid expansion of population, as the Industrial Revolution spread, but fortunately there was an accompanying increase in the understanding of the dangers to health that resulted from bad sanitation. Alternative methods of disposing of the dead had then to be considered, first cemeteries (that is to say, secular burial places) were provided by local authorities but these proved to be only temporary alleviants of a much greater problem.

Hence the idea of cremation was brought out of the past, only to be utterly rejected in horror by most people. Nevertheless in 1874 a society of enthusiasts was formed in England to promote the idea; four years later its members succeeded in buying an acre of land at Woking in Surrey, near the existing cemetery. In 1882 the local council was asked to sanction the cremation there of two people, who had left specific instructions in their wills that they wanted to be cremated. The council referred the application to the Home Secretary, who refused his consent. Two years later, Dr Price, as will be seen, tried other ways of circumventing the law.

The last historic chapter of this remarkable doctor's life began in 1883, when he was already eighty-three years of age; in that year his latest female companion Gwenllian Llywelyn, the last in a long line of female comforters, gave birth to a son. It is known that over the years the doctor had fathered a number of children, but the one born in September 1883 was, as far as is known, the only boy. He was named Iesu Grist, but despite the Christian connotation, the child was regarded by his doting father as being in the true succession of Druid leaders. He saw in him someone to whom he would be able to hand over in time all that he knew about Druid priestcraft. When the boy was but five months old, however, the unthinkable and the unbearable happened and he died. The following Sunday evening, January

13th 1884 the grieving and distraught father took the frail body to the top of Caerlan Hill, in a field behind his house, poured paraffin over it and set it alight; his neighbours, on their way home from the Sunday evening service at the nearby chapel saw the flames, rushed up the hill and snatching the half-consumed body from the flames, sent for the police. Fortunately for the chances of Dr Price's survival the police were very soon on the scene, soon enough to rescue the doctor from his enraged neighbours who would probably have thrown him on the fire. The police took him off to the police station, where he was held in custody for his own safety. An inquest was held at which Dr Price was exonerated and thereafter allowed to go home by the police. The next day a police request to the coroner to release the body of the child for them to bury was resisted by the father who persuaded the coroner to give him custody of the remains of his child. Shortly afterwards Price received a summons to appear at Cardiff Assizes to answer a charge of cremating the dead body of a child.

The scene at the assize court was a truly remarkable one; the old, grief-stricken doctor, who had thumbed his nose at the law for more than half a century, had now to stand in the dock to answer this serious charge. This was the scenario, but if onlookers expected to see a chastened old man, they were most certainly disappointed. As counsel for the defence, representing himself as he had always done in the past, Dr Price must have looked really magnificent, having most carefully arrayed himself for the big occasion. He decked himself out in a white linen smock with a bright tartan shawl thrown around his shoulders. By this time the long, black hair which had been such a feature of his appearance in former times, had been replaced by a mane of gleaming white. All in all he set himself up as an archdruid in all his glory. Mr Justice Stephen must have been suitably impressed, if not by the prisoner's appearance, at least by his eloquence and by the cogency of his arguments. After due consideration, the learned judge decided that it was legal to burn a dead body instead of burying it, as long as no offence was given to the public and provided that no criminal act was thereby committed. From that moment, with or without the consent of the Home Secretary, cremation became legal.

Dr William Price was of course jubilant as well he might have been, especially as he received a great many letters from far and near, congratulating him on his notable achievement in getting cremation legalised. To commemorate the event he even went so far as to have three thousand bronze medallions struck, which he proceeded to sell at three pence each. On March 21st 1884, two months after the conflagration on Caerlan Hill, Price once more took his dead child up the hill and completed the cremation, without any interference from his neighbours. Following Mr Justice Stephen's judgement in Cardiff, on March 26th 1885 the first cremation took place in England, when a woman's body was cremated in Woking.

If William Price had been a character in fiction, as his quite extraordinary life made him appear to be, his author would probably have made him die on the morrow of his great triumph in the law court, with his laurels still fresh upon his brow. In fact this doughty old fighter had another nine years to live, years in which he fathered two more children, carried on with his medical practice, espoused the cause of the unmarried mother and made detailed arrangements for his own eventual cremation. His daughter Penelope was born in 1886, to be followed three years later by her younger brother, another Iesu Grist, born when his father was in his ninetieth year.

The end came in January 1893, shortly before his ninety-third birthday. Early in the New Year he had been able to see patients, but a fall caused him to take to his bed. One evening he awoke from sleep and complained of being thirsty. He spurned the proffered glass of cider and asked for champagne. Indeed his last words were 'Give me champagne', which seem fitting last words for a man who drank the cup of life to the full. He died almost at once. There was a considerable flurry of excitement in Llantrisant thereafter when the news was broken; everyone knew about the arrangements for the cremation and everyone greatly looked forward to this memorable occasion. Every detail had been planned well in advance by the old man and the family saw to it that his wishes were properly carried out. The cremation took place on January 31st 1893, the venue being, of course, the top of Caerlan Hill, which twenty thousand people climbed in order to witness the first legal cremation in Wales; they had all to obtain in advance a specially printed ticket, which authorised the bearer to be admitted to the hill, where this vast crowd greatly enjoyed the astonishing sight of an iron coffin grow white as its fire of several tons of best Welsh coal took firm hold of the old doctor's earthly remains.

Readers may be interested to know that nearly a hundred years later enough people remembered the achievements of Dr Price to subscribe to a statue, which was erected in the Bull Ring at Llantrisant. On a May morning in 1982 a large crowd gathered to witness the unveiling and to join in the lusty singing of a song, specially written for the occasion and sung to the tune of God Bless The Prince of Wales. At the foot of the statue are these words. DR WILLIAM PRICE (1800 - 1893). SURGEON, CHARTIST, SELF-STYLED DRUID.

A POOR PARISH PRIEST
The white cross in the photograph marks the grave of John Price, the
Welsh country parson who chose to live in squalid seclusion in the
Radnorshire hills until he was unwittingly marked down for
recognition when he opened his door on the third of July 1872 to the
Victorian diarist, Kilvert.

Chapter 17

A Poor Parish Priest

After the astonishing twists and turns of William Price's bizarre life it seems desirable to continue on a quieter note with a brief account of one of his contemporaries, another Price, John, a gentle, unassuming country parson who professionally achieved no eminence whatsoever and would probably have died and been altogether forgotten but for a meeting one July day in 1872 on the Radnorshire hills with the Victorian diarist, Kilvert. This saintly rather ineffective priest however was no pillar of the Establishment; he was indeed a genuine eccentric, whom Kilvert always referred to as The Solitary.

The strange story of John Price is set in what is today called Powys; yesterday, so to speak, the area was known as Maesyfed, which the English, after the Act of Union in 1536, christened Radnorshire, while further back, when the Normans came to impose their unwanted sway, its name had been Elfael. Here in the nineteenth century rural life was for the most part blissfully untouched by the alarums and excursions of war or by the social changes that inevitably had followed in the train of the French Revolution ad the Napoleonic adventure. John Price, born in 1810, was to spend thirty-six peaceful though sometimes difficult and always penurious years ministering to the needs of a sparse congregation in the remote unchanged Radnorshire countryside; he finally laid aside his very shabby cassock in 1895.

In the hope that some readers of this book may want to see for themselves the delectable country where John Price had his church and his various tumble-down homes, some topographical details now follow. If the motorist moves westwards from Leominster in Herefordshire on the A44, he will have to turn left three miles west of Kington, on to the B4594; this road is fingerposted PAINSCASTLE which is ten miles further on. As the pleasant country road nears the village, it grows ever narrower and becomes a green lane, which eventually opens up to reveal PAINSCASTLE, seemingly amounting today to little more than a crossroads, a triangular green, a handful of houses and a high green mound up a lane behind a farm. Over this place for many a century loomed first a prehistoric strong point, then a wooden castle and later a stout stone fortress. Here for eight weeks in the summer of 1231 Henry III held court.

The mound on which a massive castle once dominated the landscape is largely hidden today by the two farms that come between its eroded ramparts and the village. All is change; the hand of man is slowly withdrawing from the scene. The one remaining inn was recently gutted in a fire; there is a Baptist chapel, but of a village church there is no trace. Indeed there has never been a village church in Painscastle; those who wished to worship according to the rites of the Established Church had and still have to go a mile and a half down the road to the west to Llanbedr, whose full name is Llanbedr Painscastle. A right-hand turn off this western road leads in a short distance to John Price's church, which stands to the west of the lane and almost opposite a farm. When Kilvert first saw the church in 1865, he described it in his diary as a romantic ruin, but this neglected, though still consecrated, building received a new roof in 1879, along with considerable interior refurbishment.

Son of a Welsh yeoman farmer, John Price was ordained in 1834, after leaving Queen's College, Cambridge; in the following twenty-five years he held six Welsh curacies before acquiring the living at Llanbedr in 1859. There was no vicarage and the stipend was minimal. Whether or not the local talk is true that in early days in Llanbedr he actually lived in three superannuated bathing-machines, crudely joined together, he certainly lived in various humble and unorthodox places, which no archdeacon will ever have succeeded in locating! When Kilvert tracked him down in 1872 in a hovel on Llanbedr Hill, he lived in appalling squalor. Kilvert thus describes the Solitary as he opened the door to him. 'He was a man rather below the middle height, about sixty years of age, his head covered with a luxuriant growth of light brown hair and his face made remarkable by a mild thoughtful melancholy blue eye and red moustache and white beard.'

The inside offered a challenge to the diarist as he surveyed the absolute filth around him; the stone floor was deeply piled with an accumulation of dirt and peat dust, while the only recognisable furniture consisted of two wooden chairs, one of which lacked a back, and a dressing-table covered with an assortment of plates, cups, saucers and glasses, all of which had long escaped being washed. There was no fire in the grate and everywhere there was a noxious smell. Yet, despite these intimidating surroundings, John Price had succeeded in devising and perfecting and indeed getting published a method of shorthand, the efficacy of which he there and then demonstrated to Kilvert, who was much impressed. This seems to have been Kilvert's only meeting with the Solitary, although another entry in his diary three years later commented on an accident that had befallen the hermit in his hut in the hills. Apparently he had fallen into the fire and been very badly burned. For three weeks he had to miss taking the services at Llanbedr but neither doctor nor nurse managed to gain admission to his cottage.

Around such a character legends were bound to crystallise. It seems that in an attempt to increase his meagre congregation he invited tramps to come to church and agreed to pay them sixpence every time one of them came to service. In consequence his congregation grew much larger, with the result that Price found it a financial strain to continue with the sixpenny subsidy. Meanwhile he allowed his visitors to bring their stoves into the church to cook their Sunday meal which he sometimes shared with them in a nearby barn. In time he had to inform the tramps that he proposed to reduce their present to four pence; the decision met with resistance, as the tramps withdrew to the churchyard to consider the offer! Reluctantly they gave in but, when at a later date the poor vicar tried to reduce it to threepence, the vagrants refused to agree! What effect their refusal to accept the further cut had on church attendance is unfortunately not known. It is known, however, that in an effort to raise the moral standards of this section of his congregation, he agreed to marry the tramps free of charge. In addition he gave to each couple the sum of five shillings. Report has it that thereafter some couples managed to get themselves married up to six times by suitably changing their names! Searches in the marriage entries in the parish register provided no evidence to confirm this story.

This remarkable man signed his last death certificate on March 9th 1895 just two weeks before his own death; that he lived to be eighty-five is perhaps astonishing when the long years of solitary hardship are remembered. He is buried in a grave, marked with a white cross near the south door of the church. As late as 1967 there was still alive in the parish an old couple, then in their mid-nineties, who could remember him. Their comment was: 'He was small of stature, a perfect gentleman and kindly disposed.'

ONE-NIGHT HOUSES

Tŷ Hyll is familiar to countless motorists as they speed along the A5 a mile or so to the west of Betws-y-coed. The Ugly House is now the headquarters of the Snowdonia National Park Society, which acquired it in 1988. As readers of this chapter will learn, the Ugly House began life as a one-night house in the fifteenth century; since then it has had a chequered but continuous history, its high point being possibly reached between 1815 and 1821 when Thomas Telford followed up the building of the Waterloo Bridge in Betws-y-coed by building another bridge over the river Llugwy, which was close enough to the Ugly House for some of Telford's work-force to move in there to take advantage of its relative comfort after suffering the hardships of living in Telford's tents.

Chapter 18

One-Night Houses

In all early societies land hunger was a grim reality; men needed somewhere to live and somewhere to grow their food. Wales in the early part of the Middle Ages was no exception, though in Wales this hunger was for a time partly assuaged by tribal arrangements, which very often enabled modest parcels of land to be allocated to even the poorest members of a tribal group. When however in 1536 Wales was annexed by England, the last vestiges of tribal law crumbled and with it ended the lowly peasant's meagre allocation of land. Land hunger thereafter returned and indeed later even increased when the system of enclosures became the accepted procedure. Many parts of Wales were largely uninhabited and thus escaped the attention of those who favoured the enclosing of land; in such districts an interesting 'ad hoc' practice developed, which acquired the name of One-Night-Houses. This practice over the years developed whereby a man, almost always in a remote area and thus well away from the prying eyes and sensitive ears of authority, was able, in the hours of darkness between sunset and sunrise to build for himself a minimal dwelling, consisting of one room downstairs and one room up. Such a flimsy structure became his property, according to accepted custom, if by sunrise smoke was seen to be emerging from a hole in the roof.

Custom also allowed, it appeared, not only for the building materials required for this enterprise to be gathered together beforehand but also for a party of helpful volunteers to be enlisted to speed up the endeavour. Normally the walls consisted of substantial blocks of stone and the roof was made of large turves. In areas, however, where suitable stones were in short supply, the walls too could be made of large turves, which even in modern times have been found to be well-insulated against the elements, as building experiments at the Centre for Alternative Technology near Machynlleth have proved. Generally such one-night houses were built on what was believed to be common land, but occasionally, when an absentee land-owner discovered that a one-night structure had been put up on his land, he could claim the right to demand rent, if he could prove that it had been built within the previous twelve years. Apparently however this was by no means a common occurrence.

On the morning after the busy night of frantic building the practice grew for the new house-holder to stand outside his little house, axe in hand; there in the presence of his fellow helpers, he proceeded to hurl the axe as far as he could to all four points of the compass. Where the axe fell marker posts were erected, later to be joined together by some distinctive if flimsy fencing. Thus traditionally the boundaries of a new property were established.

In later years the enclosure movement which lasted well into the nineteenth century frequently caused problems to the owners of one-night houses. Title-deeds were sometimes required from the owners, which very few of them would have been able to produce. The building of these tiny houses seems to have been most common in the eighteenth and nineteenth centuries, according to the Report of the Royal Commission on Land in Wales; which was published in 1896. The opinion was there expressed that the building of one-night houses appeared to have been 'sanctioned by public opinion'. In the course of the second half of the nineteenth century the migration of peasants in search of work in the newly-industrialised towns seems to have eased somewhat the problem of land hunger, though in remote districts in Wales the practice of building such homes seems occasionally to have taken place almost within living memory. Sometimes even today a second glance at an old Welsh cottage, if the district be hilly and remote enough, may reveal that today's exterior walls may cover an earlier primitive building, originally thrown up in one night! No eye-witness account of the actual building of such a house has come down to us, but we must surmise that the time chosen for the enterprise was left to as late as possible in the year. A dry spell late in October might well have been popular!

In the second half of the nineteenth century many one-night houses were still being lived in remote, hilly parts of Merioneth; indeed it would not be past all likelihood that a few still survive, where they may have been suitably built upon to make habitation possible.

Two examples of one-night houses follow, one from the late Middle Ages and the other from the late nineteenth century.

All motorists familiar with north Wales will have noticed the Ugly House (TŶ HYLL, which in addition to meaning Ugly House also means A ROUGH or RUGGED HOUSE, which seems more appropriate here); it stands north of the A5, a few miles west of Betws-y-coed on the way to Capel Curig. This is indeed a remarkable dwelling with a long and fascinating history. Today happily it belongs to the Snowdonia National Park Society, which has, since 1988, when it bought it, lavished much skill and money on its preservation. The Society has also produced a brochure, which outlines its remarkable story; readers are strongly advised to visit the Ugly House, go inside and buy a copy of this brochure, to which your author is much indebted.

According to legend, this strange-looking house began life as a one-night house in 1475, just ten years before Welsh Henry Tudor made his historic way through Wales northwards from Pembrokeshire en route to mounting a challenge to Richard III for the throne of England at Bosworth. Its builders are thought to have been two brothers, who had been declared outlaws. It cannot be suggested however that the massive boulders of today were put in position by these outlaws. Here as elsewhere in Wales the original walls will have been strengthened by later residents. It is known for instance that some of the workers who in the year of Waterloo helped to build the A5 west of Betws-y-coed, lived for a while in the Ugly House which with all its limitations was thought far preferable to the tents, which Thomas Telford had provided for his contracted labour.

Back to the twentieth century where a few miles up in the hilly countryside to the east of Church Stretton there lives today in retirement a very interesting Welshman Garnie Jones possessed of an enquiring mind, who spent his boyhood in Radnorshire, in the hamlet of Llanfihangel Helygen, less than five miles north of Llandrindod. His retentive memory, allied to a keen understanding, makes him ready, with only a little prompting to talk about what he remembered from his Radnorshire past. The author first enjoyed the company of Garnie Jones one evening more than twenty years ago, when he sat in our kitchen, after helping my wife to patch up our ramshackle greenhouse; he told us that he could well remember a one-night-house in his part of Radnorshire. On another occasion recently, in the late summer of 1997, I called on him and reminded him of that earlier evening. His memory still as clear as before, he proceeded to answer all my questions with the result that a fuller picture now emerges. Apparently, the one-night-house that he had talked about twenty years previously had been built by his great grandfather on common land. His grandmother, the builder's daughter, whom my informant well remembered, had lived and died in the house, which consisted of just one room up and one room down. The walls, like the roof, were made of heavy turves. The cottage is still marked on the Ordnance Survey map but though the name remains, nothing of the structure has survived, save in the memory of one Radnorshire man, who in his boyhood ran in and out of the house.

Chapter 19

Travellers' Tales

Giraldus Cambrensis (1146-1223) loved a story almost as much as did the great Greek historian Herodotus. He told how the celebrated sixth century Christian missionary and scholar Illtud at one time chose to live as a hermit in Breconshire at Llanhamlach, which lies between Brecon and Lake Llangorse. The recluse's provisions, it appeared, were always taken to him by a mare 'which became gravid after being covered by a stag, and gave birth to a creature which could run very fast, its front part being like that of a horse and its haunches resembling those of a deer'. If this story seems far-fetched to readers, they should consider how the Victorian diarist Kilvert saw fit to report in his diary on July 22nd 1871 that the local blacksmith's wife had told him that there lived in Presteigne a Miss Sylvester, 'the woman frog . . . her head and face, her eyes and mouth are those of a frog and she has a frog's legs and feet . . . she never goes out except to the Primitive Methodist Chapel . . . she is a very good person'.

Readers in the Brecon area may care to know of a legend attached to the church at Llanfaes, which is now practically a part of Brecon. Very close to the nineteenth century church is the site of a medieval place of worship, also dedicated to St David, which, according to Giraldus, was the scene in his lifetime of a remarkable occurrence.

'A boy tried to steal some young pigeons from a nest in the church, but his hand stuck fast to the stone on which he was leaning . . . for three days and nights the boy, accompanied by his parents and his friends offered vigils, fasts and prayers. On the third day, (sic) by God's intervention, the power which held his hand fast was loosened and he was released from the miraculous force which bound him to the stone. I myself saw this same boy, then no longer young, living in Newbury in England. . . . the stone is preserved to this day among the relics of the church in question, with the marks of the boy's fingers pressed into the flint as though in wax and clearly visible.'

Another traveller was JOHN LELAND (1506-1552). He was Librarian and Chaplain to Henry VIII, who in 1533 ordered him to take a journey round the whole of England and Wales to find out how much the various religious houses were worth. While staying at the Cistercian Abbey at Strata Florida in the course of investigating the neighbourhood, Leland told of an experience which had befallen a local lead-miner. This man, it seemed, had made a pet of a crow, who one day ungratefully flew off with his master's purse, just as he was about to join a shift down the mine. The miner at once gave chase over the moors but when later on he made his way back to the mine he discovered that in his absence the walls of the mine had caved in and all his colleagues on his shift had been killed.

Earlier while passing through Radnorshire he had noted down that in New Radnor the wild flower, bloodwort grew profusely in the yard of the ruined castle, a circumstance explained by local residents as being due to the sad fact that at the time of Owain Glyndŵr's rising sixty men had been beheaded there. What Leland may not have known was that bloodwort, generally known as yarrow, traditionally was associated with battlefields, because apparently the juice from the plant was efficacious in staunching the blood of wounds.

On his way back Leland passed through Denbighshire, where he commented thus . . . 'there is in the parish of Llansannan in the side of a stony hill a place where there be twenty four holes or circular places for men to sit, but some less and some bigger, cut out of the main rock by men's hands . . . their children and young men coming to seek their cattle used to sit and play . . . some called it the round table . . . '

William Camden (1551-1623), a Londoner, educated at Oxford and later Head Master of Westminster School, became the foremost antiquary in the reign of Elizabeth. His greatest achievement was the writing of BRITANNIA, in which Wales figured prominently. For all his objective and scholarly observations, however, when he visited Llanddewi Brefi, he succumbed to the temptation of claiming the authority of reliable Welsh sources for the account of a synod, which took place outdoors in the churchyard at Llanddewi Brefi. At this synod the youthful St David, a delegate, had spoken with such eloquence, vehemence and persuasiveness that the very ground on which David was standing 'mounted up to a hillock under his feet'.

Pride of place as a provider of travellers' tales as well as a chronicler of the Welsh should perhaps be given to Thomas Pennant (1726-1798). For instance, when he was being shown family portraits in a manor house in the Clwydian hills, he paid particular attention to the portrait of a lady 'exceedingly celebrated in this part of Wales'. At her husband's funeral, Pennant was told by his host, she was led to the church door by a local knight and later escorted back from the church by another local squire who 'whispered to her his wish of becoming her second (husband)'. She refused him with great civility, letting him know that she had already accepted the proposal that Sir Richard had made to her on her way to church. She assured him, however, that in case she had to repeat the same sad duty which she was then about, he might depend on it as 'being her third', to which Pennant added the comment: 'She was as good as her word'.

After leaving Denbigh Pennant called at another manor house, that of a friend who offered to let him have a look through his family papers; he thereupon had a most enjoyable time, rummaging through his host's family history, where he discovered that the present owner was the descendant of one, who in the reign of Richard III had been thwarted in his desire to marry a certain woman, whom her parents had selected for another man. However the disappointed suitor waylaid the newly-wedded couple as they left the church after the ceremony, killed the groom on the spot and carried off the dead man's wife and married her the same day. Pennant added this comment: 'She was a maid, widow and wife twice in one day.'

On another occasion, while touring Snowdonia, he produced a thumb-nail sketch of a local character, a woman, who lived near Llyn Peris above Llanberis near the ruins of Dolbadarn Castle. Her name was Margaret uch Evan, who at that time (1786) was about ninety years of age. 'This extraordinary female was the greatest hunter, shooter and fisher of her time . . . she kept a dozen dogs, greyhounds, terriers and spaniels . . . she killed more foxes in one year than all the hunts did in ten . . . she rowed stoutly . . . fiddled excellently . . . knew all our old music . . . she was a very good joiner and at the age of seventy was the best wrestler in the country . . . Margaret was also a blacksmith, a shoe-maker and a maker of harps. She shoed her own horses and built her own boats, while she was under contract to carry the copper ore down the lakes'. By way of footnote, it has to be added that she died in 1801 aged 105.

In his *Wild Wales*, which reported on his foot journey through Wales in 1854, George Borrow (1803-1881) afforded readers their last chance of seeing Wales before the full effects of the Industrial Revolution made themselves manifest. The eight-mile walk from Swansea to Neath proved to be a revelation to him. 'As I proceeded I soon passed pleasant groves and hedgerows, sometimes huge works; in this valley there was a singular mixture of nature and art, of the voices of birds and the clanking of chains, of the mists of heaven and the smoke of furnaces . . . at a distance, about a quarter of a mile, stood, looking darkly grey, a ruin of vast size, with window holes, towers, spires and arches. Between it and the vast pandemonium lay a horrid, filthy place, part of which was swamp, part pool, the pool, black with soot and the swamp of a disgusting leaden colour . . . so strange a scene I had never beheld in nature.' That was Neath Abbey, one of the most famous Cistercian abbeys of Wales.

On almost the last stage of his journey, on the road from Merthyr Tydfil to Caerphilly, Borrow had a bizarre encounter with a truly remarkable Irish woman, who 'seemed between forty and fifty, was bare-footed and bare-headed, with grizzled hair hanging in elf-locks, and was dressed in rags and tatters. When about ten yards from me, she pitched forwards, gave three or four grotesque tumbles, heels over head, then standing bolt upright about a yard before me, she raised her right arm and shouted in a most discordant voice, 'Give me an alms for the glory of God.' Borrow, as always, wanting to know more, made his offer of alms dependent on receiving more information, to the giving of which he had to listen, while she unveiled an alleged sequence of events, to which readers are referred for their entertainment rather than enlightenment! Finally Borrow gave her a shilling, whereupon 'giving two or three grotesque topples she hurried away in the direction of Merthyr Tydfil.'

A Gorsedd ceremony at the National Eisteddfod at the beginning of the 20th century, during Hwfa Môn's term as Archdruid.

Chapter 20

Eisteddfodau down the Ages

Every year in the first week of August all those intimately involved in strengthening and perpetuating the culture of Wales meet in session at the National Eisteddfod, which is held in the north and south of the country in alternate years. It has now become one of the great folk festivals of Europe; it is a national pageant with its roots deeply buried in Wales' Celtic past. The compére of the main ceremonies is called the Archdruid, and the Gorsedd, the assembly of bards whose members are attired in ceremonial robes reminiscent of what are generally believed to have been worn by Druids in the long ago. In addition to this national Eisteddfod there has blossomed in recent years a great international Eisteddfod at Llangollen, while there are few parts of Wales which do not boast of a local eisteddfod of varying sizes and varying degrees of cultural significance.

Our vague and therefore unsatisfactory knowledge of Druid beliefs and culture is partly due to the savagery with which Roman soldiers destroyed the Druid headquarters in Anglesey in AD61 and partly because the Druids themselves, the leaders of a jealously maintained hierarchy, saw to it that their priests maintained the utmost secrecy about their beliefs, insisting that all teaching and indoctrination should be transmitted solely by word of mouth. Folk memory in the succeeding centuries however must have secured the transmission from one generation to another of some part of the Druid heritage, because in 1284 Edward Ist thought it necessary to do all he could to suppress Druidism in Wales.

That there were bards at work in Wales in the Middle Ages is beyond question; devoted scholars carried on certain traditions, which governed the activities of poets and musicians. Readers are reminded of the numerous references to these cultural activities in Giraldus Cambrensis' twelfth century book, Description of Wales. It is known too that from at least the twelfth century there had existed, especially in Gwynedd, a body of men who made it their business occasionally to meet together in order to set standards of excellence to which poets and musicians had to aspire. To this end competitions were organised, which must have in essence resembled the eisteddfods of later centuries. There is no record of any frequent or continual calling of such assemblies but there is documentary proof of a successful eisteddfod being held at Caerwys in the sixteenth century and of another, particularly successful meeting taking place at Corwen in 1789.

At this point Iolo Morganwg, whose sabbatical year has already been described to readers in Chapter 15, again played an important part in the story, because in 1791, fortified by his return to freedom, his batteries fully recharged, he conceived the idea of restoring Druidism to Wales, announcing his own claim to be the last surviving Druid bard. In this year, he made a second visit to London, where he hoped to have published further books. His wife and two children were left behind in an impoverished state in Wales. Back in London he renewed his former contacts only to find that in his absence he had become a man of some standing in the capital. He succeeded in joining the Society of the Gwyneddigion, whose membership, as its name implies, was mostly recruited from exiles from north Wales. He found the company very congenial and stimulating, especially as much stress was laid upon the strong achievements of the men of Gwynedd, even going as far back as the Middle Ages.

Iolo thereafter burned with a passionate longing to do for Glamorgan what these Gwynedd members were doing for their own part of Wales. If Gwynedd had had splendid cultural traditions back in the Middle Ages, then, he, Iolo Morganwg, was fiercely determined to do the same for his much-loved Glamorgan, even if it became necessary to involve himself in another round of literary forgeries, which before long he produced, only to pass them off to his fellow club members as genuine manuscripts, which, according to him, he had rescued from oblivion in remote corners of the valleys of Glamorgan.

At this time, the glowing spark of Iolo's Druidism was fanned into fiery flame, when he discovered in the meetings of the Gwyneddigion that there were authentic records in north Wales of long-established Druid procedures, whereby poets and musicians met periodically to compete with each other in poetry and song. These were perfectly genuine traditions of medieval eisteddfods, organised at the local level. In September 1792 Iolo made his most determined attempt to give his native Glamorgan at least cultural parity with Gwynedd. Earlier in the year a volume of Welsh poetry had been published to which Iolo had contributed an introduction in which he stressed that contemporary Welsh poets, whose work appeared in the collection, were the true descendants of the ancient Druid bards, who had sung their songs, according to Iolo, in the valleys of Glamorgan in the Middle Ages.

The publication of this book was followed by a remarkable event that took place on Primrose Hill in London on September 23rd; to that outdoor meeting Iolo had invited friends to participate in the celebration of the autumn equinox. This was the time when new styles of religious practice were being talked about, especially in France, where the French Revolution was just three years old. In devising rituals and ceremonies for this occasion Iolo, though certainly influenced by current developments in France, where revolutionaries were becoming excited about nature worship, was primarily concerned with acquiring for Glamorgan a prominent place in the cultural history of Welsh bards.

This Primrose Hill gathering in celebration of the autumn equinox gave Iolo's friends the chance to take part in a ritual, specially devised by Iolo, though he told his fellow Welshmen that in fact they were reviving an ancient Glamorgan ritual that went back to the Middle Ages. A circle of stones had been arranged in the centre of which stood a big stone, the Maen

Gorsedd, on which a sword was placed, which the members of the group proceeded together to sheathe, while all chanted fervent prayers, which of course Iolo had specially written for the occasion. This piece of preliminary ritual having been gone through to Iolo's satisfaction, a bardic competition then took place, followed by the chairing of the bard; Iolo, in inventing this chairing ceremony, was seeking to add weight to the time-honoured traditions, associated with north Wales since the Middle Ages. The circle of stones, which may in fact at Primrose Hill have consisted of little more than a handful of pebbles, was Iolo's inspired touch of ritual, which, once he had persuaded the true inheritors of Eisteddfod traditions to incorporate into their ceremonial, greatly added to Glamorgan's cultural prestige. Just how far contemporaries accepted Iolo's claim that the Primrose Hill Gorsedd was a genuine revival of an ancient Glamorgan observance is not known but it must be emphasised that, however unimportant the ceremony may have seemed at the time, the ritual which Iolo had fabricated for the occasion is today an integral part of the National Eisteddfod.

Iolo Morganwg however can hardly be given the credit for the considerable growth in popularity and status of the National Eisteddfod in the early years of the 19th century. New ideas had helped to produce revolution in America in the 1770s, ideas which in their turn crossed back to Europe, where they were greatly to influence attitudes towards fundamental change, which took place in France in the 1790s. This new intellectual excitement also showed itself this side of the Channel, and in Wales gave added impetus to a national cultural awakening, which was to find expression in the acceptance of the idea of a national Eisteddfod. Of this new mental awareness Iolo was to take advantage. A friendship developed between him and Thomas Burgess, the Bishop of St David's, which bore fruit in an eisteddfod held in Carmarthen in 1819.

The Cambrian Society of Dyfed organised the event, which

was held in the Ivy Bush Hotel and lasted for three days. Iolo, now an old man of 72, and ailing, but a much respected figure, had been invited and indeed on the third day made a notable intervention in the proceedings, when he persuaded the Bishop of St David's and the other important officials to bring the affairs of the eisteddfod to a climax with the chairing of the bard. Having gained the necessary assent and having taken from his pocket small stones with which he made a circle in the garden of the hotel, the first Gorsedd, the first Chairing of the Bard took place as a recognised part of an eisteddfod. The continuing ceremonial rituals associated with this national event constitute Iolo's most abiding memorial.

Successful eisteddfods followed the Carmarthen meeting; they were held respectively at Caernarfon in 1821, at Brecon in 1822 and in Welshpool in 1824. As the century advanced however with the inevitable and overspeedy industrialisation in the valleys of the south and the coalfields of the north-east of the country talk of change was in the air, even in the conduct of the National Eisteddfod, where a great increase in competitiveness soon became general. It seems however that one feature remained inviolate, the supremacy of the competition for the best long poem in Welsh in a strict metre on a specified topic. Whereas winners of other competitions were crowned, the poet of the best poem in strict verse was chaired. He/she received the supreme honour, becoming the champion of champions. One further fact about the eisteddfod has to be added for the benefit of non-Welsh readers, the insistence on all competitions being conducted in the Welsh language. With all the stress laid on the outstanding need to strengthen Welsh culture, its underlying purpose is to increase the use of the Welsh language, which, in the words of Jan Morris 'is the truest badge of Welsh identity'.

It seems fitting to end this chapter on Welsh eisteddfods with a reference to another National Eisteddfod held in Llangollen, where in 1858 a song submitted as an entry was taken up and sung with very great enthusiasm by the audience.

This song had been written two years previously in Pontypridd, its joint authors being father and son, Evan James (Ieuan ap Iago) and James James. They were both weavers in a local mill where father Evan busied his mind with poetic ideas while his fingers nimbly plied the loom, as he wove Welsh flannel, while James also divided his attention as he worked in the same mill, but while his father's bent was for poetry, his son tended to express himself in musical terms. It is believed that father Evan was first in the field with the words, but in the absence of firm evidence hearsay hardened into accepted fact that the miraculous marriage of words and music came about one memorable Sunday afternoon in 1856, when father and son foregathered in the family home in Pontypridd. Thus it was that 'Mae hen wlad fy nhadau' (*Land of my fathers* to the English) came into being. Words and Music, thus happily fused together into song, slowly went into local circulation; it is believed that it was first sung in public in a Methodist chapel in Maesteg. Certainly it was sung two years later at the National Eisteddfod in Llangollen, and it was first published in 1860. Evan died in 1878, seven years before it was officially accepted as the National Anthem. His son James lived on into the 20th century, dying in 1902, by which time his music was known and loved throughout the country. In Pontypridd today there stands a bronze statue commemorating the achievements of these local weavers.

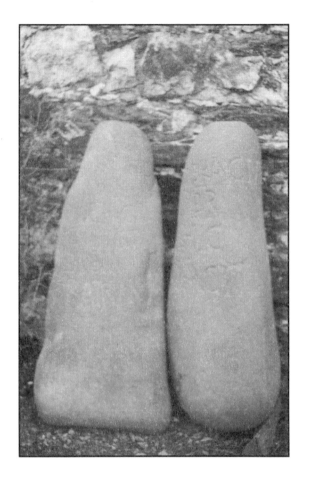

ANELOG STONES

These historic stones, now in the safe keeping of St Hywyn's church in
Aberdaron, marked the graves of two priests in the monastery grounds
at Anelog, GR 156274, about a mile north-west of Aberdaron.
These gravestones of Veracius and Senacus are the silent witnesses
of a very early Christian settlement in the Llŷn peninsula.

Chapter 21

The Magic of the Llŷn Peninsula

What constitutes magic is open to much debate; to the author there are several parts of Wales that continually hold him in thrall, but the Llŷn Peninsula was the first to have this magical effect on him, an effect that has stood the test of many years of intermittent visiting. Delving further into memory there was one particular magnet that first drew him into the area and when that magnet had worked its spell, it was succeeded by another, operating in the opposite direction, which continued to draw him back to the Llŷn again and again, as it still does, even or perhaps especially in old age.

This first magnet was the Pilgrims' route which operated westwards from Clynnog Fawr and the second, an even stronger one, was the tip of the peninsula, around Aberdaron and, what lay beyond, the sacred island of Bardsey. Experience, we are taught, is what one finds when looking for something else, and so it has proved to be in Llŷn, where a search for a well or a cairn or an inscribed stone has occasionally led to the revelation of a rare flower or a bird's nest or better still, to an unexpected conversation with a man or woman who then guided me to other unsuspected treasures in this remarkable landscape.

The footprints of the past are everywhere to be seen hereabouts: a Neolithic burial-place, Bronze Age monuments, the Iron Age splendours to be found on Tre'r Ceiri, Latin inscriptions on early Christian tombstones, erected a century and more before St Augustine set foot in Kent, ancient wells, early non-conformist chapels, incomparable stretches of coast-line – all the constituents of a magic land, and, with all its treasures, the peninsula is greater than the sum-total of its parts. Bardsey seems to have cast its own potent, peaceful spell upon the land.

One man's sample of various places of interest to be found in this enchanted land would certainly include the following.

Ffynnon Gybi (G.R. 429413)

This well in central Llŷn, east of the A499, which links Llanaelhaearn with Pwllheli will be found a short distance north-east of the parish church of Llangybi. This ancient well had a long history of curing all manner of misfortunes from warts to blindness and rheumatism, when in 1750 a Mr William Price saw fit to build a bath and a bath-house at the well. So popular did this little spa become that its miraculous water was taken away in casks and bottles to be used as medicine. An eel, alleged to lie in the bottom of the well, was not only believed to speed up cures but also played a significant role in certain rituals connected with the cures; for instance, patients at one time were encouraged to stand bare-legged in the well and if the eel coiled itself around the patients' legs, it was interpreted as a sure sign that a cure had begun. In the well's heyday in the second half of the eighteenth century a doctor pronounced that the well-water contained important mineral properties.

Memorial Stone at Llangian (G.R. 295289)

Llangian lies two miles north-west of Abersoch on the south coast of Llŷn; in the south side of the churchyard, a short distance from the church, is a sixth century memorial stone, which at one time had a sun-dial erected on top of it. The three holes, through which the dial was formerly held in position, are still visible and help in identifying the grave, which over the years has suffered very badly indeed from erosion. When Nash-Williams first identified the Latin inscription on the east face of the stone, the lettering was clear; today this is no longer true and it is only possible to read it if the light is right. It is worth time and trouble to find this stone, because it marks the grave of the first doctor known in Wales. The inscription reads MELI MEDICI FILI MARTINI IACIT (Dr Melius, the son of Martin, lies here). As the pilgrim exodus from north-east Wales to

Bardsey is believed to have begun in the sixth century, it is not too fanciful to surmise that this Dr Melius may well have attended pilgrims in need – the nearest point to the pilgrim route is Llangwnnadl, which is about seven miles north-west of Llangian.

Pistyll Church (G.R. 328423)

For those who want to get nearer the lives of former pilgrims, a visit is recommended to Pistyll, whose little church is reached via a minor road, shortly before the main road B4417 from Llanaelhaearn reaches the village of Pistyll. Beyond the church is a farm today, on the site of an early monastery, whose responsibilities included attending to the needs of pilgrims, most of whom will have rested in a twenty acre field nearby, reserved for their special use. The all-important fish-pond may be seen on the other side of the little road from the church, which, dedicated to St Beuno, was of medieval origin, occupying the same site as the original pilgrim church, whose walls were made of wood and roof of thatch. On the steep slope of the mound on which the church and churchyard stand may still be found, in season, all manner of berry-bearing shrubs, the probable descendants of the bushes which supplied the needs of the pilgrims. Also in the churchyard medicinal herbs have survived from the middle ages. An annual pilgrimage was revived in 1950, on the pilgrim route, as a result of which historically-minded traditionalists have since then three times a year, at Easter, Lammas and at Christmas, strewn rushes on the church floor and tied up in the nave bunches of medicinal herbs and other plants gathered from the churchyard.

Capel Newydd, Nanhoron (G.R. 287309)

This chapel, despite its name, is the oldest nonconformist chapel in north Wales, having been converted from a barn by Congregationalists in 1769. Would-be visitors should note that it is hidden away in a field, south of Nanhoron village; if Nanhoron is approached from the north on the B4413, drive through the village, and about half a mile further on in a south-easterly direction a house will be seen on the right-hand side, in the garden of which a notice indicates that the chapel lies about two hundred yards down a green lane to the side of the house, in whose keeping is the huge iron key of the chapel. The lane is passable in a small car but is not recommended.

Here in 1769 Congregationalists converted a barn for their use, the floor is still earthen, though the very large stones on the floor of the box pews protected worshippers' feet from immediate contact with the earth. These tall pews, all of them with hinged doors, covered today with bird droppings, speak of other days as also does the hand bier at the back of the chapel.

Aberdaron

The author was first made aware of the drawing power of the area around Aberdaron, when more than fifty years ago, on a sunny April day, he cycled down the last hill toward the sea; on both sides of the road the gorse was in bloom and an escort of goldfinches obligingly flew in front of us, leading us down the steep hill to our first sight of Aberdaron. No-one had adequately prepared us for the sheer excitement of that first glimpse. Nothing seems to have changed there since. Of Bardsey Island, of course, I had read but in my ignorance I was quite unaware of the great importance of Aberdaron in the early days of Christian settlement in these Celtic lands. Thereafter I discovered that from about 500 A.D. until the middle of the sixteenth century, when Henry VIII 'dissolved the monasteries', Aberdaron had enjoyed complete monastic control of the area. The earliest known monastic site in the district was at Anelog, which is about a mile north-west of Aberdaron. Some years later (not even an approximate date can be given) power passed from Anelog to Aberdaron, where St Hywyn's church stands today, on the very edge of a gently shelving beach, where so many subsequent crossings to Bardsey have since started.

Propped up against the north wall inside the chancel of

Aberdaron's parish church are two grave-stones of enormous historical interest and value. These stones bear inscriptions in Latin of two of the priests at Anelog and were discovered in the eighteenth century in the valley of the river Sant, as it flowed through Anelog on its way to the sea at Aberdaron. In recent years they have passed into the safe and proper custody of this church, one stone commemorating a priest called VERACIUS, the other, also a priest, who was named SENACUS; accompanying the name is the important added information that he was remembered along with 'many brother priests', furnishing proof of a local monastery at Anelog. When in the twelfth century Giraldus Cambrensis visited Aberdaron, he referred to two local monastic communities, the one at Aberdaron, the other on Bardsey, as will be described later.

In the middle of the village stands a white-washed house, Y GEGIN FAWR, *The Big Kitchen*; it still supplies food and drink to travellers as it has done down the years, whether they will soon pile back into their cars for the journey home or make their way on foot to the nearby beach to await sea transport to Bardsey. The present building was probably erected in the seventeenth century, but it is believed that an earlier hostelry occupied the same site since the middle ages. In today's café in a display cabinet may be seen what looks like an identity disc lost on the beach in an earlier century, while the pilgrim waited for transport to Bardsey.

There is much more to explore around Aberdaron, – to the west, the headland under Castell Odo, with its Iron Age fort, from where Bardsey is clearly visible, and again further north, at Porth Oer *(Whistling Sands)*, where the choughs are likely to outnumber human beings; east of Aberdaron overlooking Porth Neigwl *(Hell's Mouth)* is Plas-yn-Rhiw, a small and delightful manor house, lovingly rescued from neglect by Mrs Keating and her daughters before passing it on to the National Trust, who allow public access both to the house and to the splendid gardens, indeed so splendid that Plas-yn-Rhiw has now to be added to the list of outstanding attractions to be found in this part of the peninsula.

Bardsey Island *(Ynys Enlli)*

At long last Bardsey Island has been reached; it may initially prove disappointing to some, because many of the ruined buildings are uninteresting, but if there is not much to see, there is a great deal there to feel for those with sensitive antennae. Of the early history of Bardsey not very much is known for certain, although there is a well-supported tradition that the Breton Celtic Christian missionary St Cadfan, who is credited with having set up a llan in Tywyn, then moved up the coast and crossed to the island where he founded a Christian community in 516. In this same sixth century it is thought likely that this small monastic community was used as an occasional retreat by mainland monks from Anelog, like Veracius and Senacus. When a century later the infamous large-scale slaughter by Saxon soldiery of the monks at Bangor-is-coed in north-east Wales caused an exodus of surviving monks in which they moved westwards, these survivors started a pilgrim movement which was to develop for centuries via Clynnog, Llanaelhaearn, Pistyll, Nefyn and Llangwnnadl en route for Aberdaron and Bardsey.

Bardsey's peace and tranquillity were shattered in the ninth and tenth centuries when Viking raiders, having established themselves in Dublin in 853, thereafter made repeated savage raids on north Wales, raids in which Bardsey was not spared. As a result of these many assaults Ynys Enlli began to be known by its Viking name, Bardsey. After the passing of this scourge a Christian community, probably Celtic in nature, began again to flourish.

This will have been the Christian community referred to by Giraldus Cambrensis when on his visit to Bardsey toward the end of the twelfth century he commented upon there being two Christian monasteries, one at Aberdaron, the other on Bardsey.

By the thirteenth century this monastic order had been taken over by the Augustinians, the foundations of whose abbey in the north of the island may still be seen (St Mary's). Giraldus made particular reference to 'the holy monks of Enlli', who were, he said, 'extremely devout' adding 'either because of the pure air or through some miracle, occasioned by the merits of the holy men, no-one died there except in extreme old age, for disease is almost unheard of'.

Since this happy time not all the inhabitants of the island have been holy men, despite the belief that twenty-thousand saints are buried in Bardsey, as, for instance, in the sixteenth century sea-pirates made their headquarters there. By the nineteenth century less than a hundred people still lived there and that number continued to dwindle in the twentieth century but better times seem to lie ahead. Today Bardsey is owned by the Bardsey Island Trust Limited, a charity, pledged to maintain the island 'as a place of natural beauty and peace and as a human community'. The island possesses an important Bird and Field Observatory, which provides accommodation for visitors. In addition spiritual retreats are arranged under the auspices of the Chapel and Retreat Committee, which advises the Island Trust on these matters.

Index

Illustrations